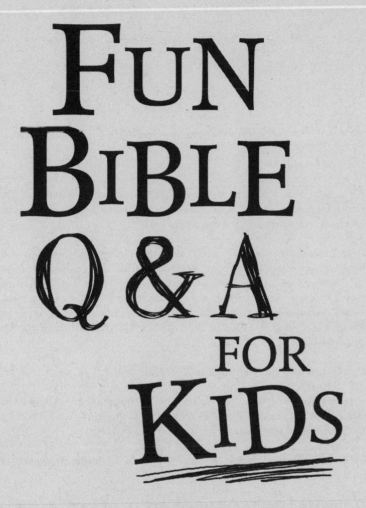

FUN BIBLE Q & A FOR KIDS

BARBOUR
PUBLISHING

© 1997 by Barbour Publishing, Inc.

ISBN 978-1-60260-861-0

Puzzles have previously appeared in *Kids' Bible Q & A*.

Scripture quotations have been paraphrased by the author, based on the HOLY BIBLE, NEW INTERNATIONAL VERSION®. NIV®. Copyright© 1973, 1978, 1984 by International Bible Society. Published by Zondervan.

Published by Barbour Publishing, Inc., P.O. Box 719, Uhrichsville, Ohio 44683, www.barbourbooks.com

Our mission is to publish and distribute inspirational products offering exceptional value and biblical encouragement to the masses.

ecpa Member of the
Evangelical Christian
Publishers Association

Printed in the United States of America.
Offset Paperback Mfrs., Inc., Dallas, PA; May 2010; D10002336

USING THE WORD LIST BELOW, FILL IN
THE BLANKS TO COMPLETE THE VERSES.

"_ _ _ _ _ IS THE PERSON
WHO DOESN'T _ _ _ _ _ _ _
TO THE WICKED. HE DOESN'T
GO WHERE _ _ _ _ _ _ _ _
GO. HE DOESN'T DO WHAT
_ _ _ PEOPLE DO. HE LOVES
THE _ _ _ _ _ TEACHINGS.
HE THINKS ABOUT THOSE
_ _ _ _ _ _ _ _ _ _
_ _ _ AND _ _ _ _ _ _."

PSALM 1:1-2

WORD LIST

TEACHINGS	LISTEN
BAD	DAY
NIGHT	SINNERS
HAPPY	LORD'S

1

HOW MUCH OF THE BIBLE DO YOU KNOW?

MATCH THE ANSWERS ON THE FOLLOWING PAGE TO THE QUESTIONS BELOW.

1. WHO SAID, "I AM WHO I AM" ?

   EXODUS 3:14

   _____

2. WHAT DID GOD CREATE ON THE FIRST DAY?

   GENESIS 1:3-5

   _____

3. WHO BUILT THE ARK?

   GENESIS 6:13-14

   _____

4. HOW MANY SONS DID NOAH HAVE ?

   GENESIS 6:10

   _____

5. WHAT WERE THE NAMES OF NOAH'S SONS ?

   GENESIS 6:10

   _____   _____   _____

6. WHO SAID, "AM I SUPPOSED TO TAKE CARE OF MY BROTHER ?"

   GENESIS 4:9

   _____

LIGHT	HAM
SHEM	JOSEPH
MOSES	NOAH
SIX	JAPHETH
GOD	CAIN
THREE	SEA

MULTIPLE CHOICE

CIRCLE THE CORRECT ANSWER.

1. WHOSE LIFE WAS SAVED BY BEING LOWERED OVER A WALL IN A BASKET?

   ACTS 9:25

   A. JOHN'S

   B. THE CRIPPLED MAN

   C. SAUL'S

2. DAVID SAID THAT GOD MADE MAN A LITTLE LOWER THAN WHAT?

   PSALM 8:5

   A. STARS

   B. ANGELS

   C. ANIMALS

3. WHERE WAS MOSES STANDING WHEN GOD TOLD HIM TO TAKE OFF HIS SHOES?

   EXODUS 3:5

   A. ON A MOUNTAIN

   B. ON HOLY GROUND

CONT'D ON NEXT PAGE...

4

4. HOW MANY DISCIPLES HAD THE NAME
   OF JAMES ?

   MATTHEW 10:2-3

      A. TWO

      B. FOUR

      C. SEVEN

5. WHAT DOES THE HEBREW WORD, "ABBA ,"
   MEAN ?

   ROMANS 8:15

      A. HELLO

      B. DADDY

      C. MOMMY

6. WHO DID JESUS SAY THE SABBATH
   WAS MADE FOR ?

   MARK 2:27

      A. GOD

      B. UNBELIEVERS

      C. MAN

MATCH THE ANSWERS

MATCH THE ANSWERS ON THE FOLLOWING
PAGE TO THE QUESTIONS BELOW.

1. WHO ASKED GOD TO SPARE SODOM?

   _____
   GENESIS 18:23-33

2. WHO WROTE FIRST AND SECOND CORINTHIANS?

   _____
   1 COR.1:1, 2 COR.1:1

3. WHO DID JESUS SAY WILL INHERIT THE
   EARTH?
   MATTHEW 5:5

   _____

4. WHAT IS THE NAME GIVEN TO JESUS
   THAT MEANS "GOD IS WITH US"?
   MATTHEW 1:23

   _____

5. WHAT WILL GOD GIVE US PLENTY OF IF
   WE ASK HIM?
   JAMES 1:5

   _____

6. WHERE IN EGYPT DID JOSEPH'S
   FAMILY LIVE?
   GENESIS 47:6

   _____

THE STRONG   PAUL

PETER   EMMANUEL

HOSANNA   ABRAHAM

MONEY   WISDOM

GOSHEN   THE MEEK

MULTIPLE CHOICE

CIRCLE THE CORRECT ANSWER.

1. WHAT WAS SARAH'S NAME BEFORE GOD CHANGED IT ?

    GENESIS 17:15

    A. SALLY

    B. HAGAR

    C. SARAI

2. WHO DID PAUL CALL HIS OWN SON ?

    1 TIMOTHY 1:1-2

    A. PETER

    B. TIMOTHY

    C. JOHN

3. WHO PREACHED ON THE DAY OF PENTECOST ?

    ACTS 2:14

    A. JOHN

    B. PAUL

    C. PETER

CONT'D ON NEXT PAGE...

4. WHAT DID JACOB WEAR TO TRICK HIS
   FATHER?
   GENESIS 27:15-24

      A. SHEEPSKIN

      B. BEARSKIN

      C. GOATSKIN

5. HOW MANY PLAGUES DID GOD BRING
   ON EGYPT?
   EXODUS 7-11

      A. SEVEN

      B. TEN

      C. TWELVE

6. WHAT WAS THE NAME OF THE WELL THAT
   THE SAMARITAN WOMAN DREW WATER
   FROM?
   JOHN 4:6-7

      A. SAMARIA WELL

      B. JOSEPH'S WELL

      C. JACOB'S WELL

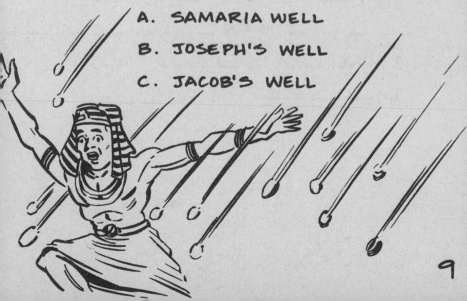

FILL IN THE BLANKS

WORD LIST	
LIFE	RESURRECTION
FOOL	WICKED
LORD	SHEPHERD
EVERYTHING	NEED

1. IN JOHN 11:25, JESUS SAID, "I AM THE _ _ _ _ _ _ _ _ _ _ _ _ _ AND THE _ _ _ _ ."

2. IN PSALM 14:1, IT SAYS, "A _ _ _ _ _ _ _ _ _ _ SAYS TO HIMSELF, 'THERE IS NO GOD'."

3. IN PSALM 23:1, IT SAYS, "THE _ _ _ _ IS MY _ _ _ _ _ _ _ _ I HAVE _ _ _ _ _ _ _ _ _ _ I _ _ _ _ ."

FILL IN THE BLANKS

WORD LIST

LIGHT	CREATED	FEMALE
SAVES	IMAGE	
PROTECTS	AFRAID	
WAY	TRUTH	
LIFE	MALE	

1. IN PSALM 27:1, IT SAYS, "THE LORD
   IS MY _____ AND THE
   ONE WHO _____ ME. I
   FEAR NO ONE. THE LORD
   _____ MY LIFE.
   I AM _____ OF NO ONE."

2. IN JOHN 14:6, JESUS SAID, "I AM THE
   ____. I AM THE _____
   AND THE ____."

3. IN GENESIS 1:27, IT SAYS, "SO GOD
   _____ HUMAN BEINGS IN
   HIS _____. IN THE IMAGE OF
   GOD HE CREATED THEM. HE CREATED
   THEM _____ AND _____."

11

MATCH THE ANSWERS

MATCH THE ANSWERS ON THE
FOLLOWING PAGE TO THE QUESTIONS
BELOW.

1. WHO WAS ISHMAEL'S MOTHER?

   GENESIS 16:15

   _____

2. WHO WAS THE FATHER OF MANY NATIONS?

   GENESIS 17:1-4

   _____

3. WHO WAS THE BROTHER OF MARTHA
   AND MARY?

   JOHN 11:1-2

   _____

4. WHAT IS THE ROOT OF ALL EVIL?

   1 TIMOTHY 6:10

   _____

5. WHAT IS THE JEWISH DAY OF REST
   CALLED?

   EXODUS 20:10

   _____

6. IN WHAT AREA IS BETHLEHEM
   LOCATED?

   MATTHEW 2:1

   _____

SARAH   ABRAHAM

ISAAC   SELFISHNESS

LOVE OF MONEY   HAGAR

LAZARUS   PETER

JERUSALEM   SABBATH

SUNDAY   JUDEA

MULTIPLE CHOICE

CIRCLE THE CORRECT ANSWER.

1. WHAT WAS THE NAME OF ABRAHAM'S PROMISED SON?

   GENESIS 21:3

   A. ISHMAEL

   B. RONALD

   C. ISAAC

2. WHAT WAS THE NAME OF JACOB'S YOUNGEST SON?

   GENESIS 35:18

   A. JOSEPH

   B. JUDAH

   C. BENJAMIN

3. WHO DID AQUILA AND PRISCILLA MEET IN CORINTH?

   ACTS 18:1-2

   A. JOHN

   B. PAUL

   C. PETER

CONT'D ON NEXT PAGE...

...CONT'D FROM PREVIOUS PAGE.

4. WHAT DID KING BELSHAZZAR SEE ON THE ?

DANIEL 5:5-8

    A. FINGER PRINTS

    B. A HAND WRITING

    C. A BUG

5. WHAT DID GOD MAKE GROW OVER JONAH TO GIVE HIM SHADE ?

JONAH 4:6

    A. A HOUSE

    B. A TREE

    C. A VINE

6. WHERE DID KING SOLOMON FIND CEDAR TREES FOR THE TEMPLE ?

1 KINGS 5:6

    A. A LUMBER STORE

    B. HIS BACK YARD

    C. LEBANON

15

MULTIPLE CHOICE

CIRCLE THE CORRECT ANSWER.

1. HOW MANY BOOKS ARE THERE IN THE BIBLE?

   A. SIXTY-EIGHT

   B. SIXTY-SIX

   C. THIRTY-FOUR

2. WHAT COMMANDMENT SAYS, "YOU MUST NOT MURDER ANYONE"?

   EXODUS 20:13

   A. TWELFTH

   B. SIXTH

   C. SEVENTH

3. HOW MANY BOOKS ARE IN THE NEW TESTAMENT?

   A. TWENTY-SIX

   B. TWENTY-EIGHT

   C. TWENTY-SEVEN

CONT'D ON NEXT PAGE...

...CONT'D FROM PREVIOUS PAGE.

4. HOW MANY FRIENDS CAME TO SPEAK
   WITH JOB?

   JOB 2:11

   A. ONE

   B. THREE

   C. THIRTY-SIX

5. ON WHICH DAY DID GOD CREATE THE
   SUN, MOON, AND STARS?

   GENESIS 1:14-19

   A. SECOND

   B. FOURTH

   C. SIXTH

6. HOW MANY TIMES DID JESUS ASK
   PETER IF HE LOVED HIM?

   JOHN 21: 15-17

   A. ONE

   B. THREE

   C. FIVE

FILL IN THE BLANKS

WORD LIST

PATIENT	TRUST	ANGRY
JEALOUS	RUDE	HOPES
TRUTH	SELFISH	WRONGS
BRAG	STRONG	HAPPY
PROUD	KIND	

" LOVE IS _____ AND

_____ . LOVE IS NOT _____ ,

IT DOES NOT _____ , AND IT IS NOT

_____ . LOVE IS NOT _____ ,

IT IS NOT _____ , AND

DOES NOT BECOME _____

EASILY. LOVE DOES NOT REMEMBER

_____ DONE AGAINST IT.

LOVE IS NOT _____ WITH

EVIL , BUT IS HAPPY WITH

_____ .

CONT'D NEXT PAGE...

18

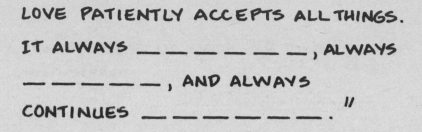

LOVE PATIENTLY ACCEPTS ALL THINGS.
IT ALWAYS _ _ _ _ _ _, ALWAYS
_ _ _ _ _, AND ALWAYS
CONTINUES _ _ _ _ _ _. "

1 CORINTHIANS 13: 4-7

THIS IS LOVE

MATCH THE ANSWERS

MATCH THE ANSWERS ON THE FOLLOWING PAGE TO THE QUESTIONS BELOW.

1. WHO SENT HIS SONS TO EGYPT TO BUY GRAIN?

   GENESIS 42:1-2

   _____

2. WHO SAID TO JESUS, "YOU ARE THE CHRIST, THE SON OF THE LIVING GOD"?

   MATTHEW 16:16

   _____

3. WHO SAID, "WHEN I NEEDED CLOTHES, YOU CLOTHED ME"?

   MATTHEW 25:36

   _____

4. HOW MANY BOOKS IN THE BIBLE ARE NAMED "JOHN"?

   _____

5. ON WHICH DAY DID GOD CREATE THE ANIMALS OF THE WATER AND THE AIR?

   GENESIS 1:20-23

   _____

6. WHAT ARE THE STORIES CALLED THAT JESUS TAUGHT BY?

   MATTHEW 13:13

   _____

FOUR	JOHN
PETER	ISAAC
JAMES	JESUS
JACOB	THREE
SIXTH	FIFTH
TALES	PARABLES

MATCH THE ANSWERS

MATCH THE ANSWERS ON THE FOLLOWING PAGE TO THE QUESTIONS BELOW.

1. WHO SOLD HIS BIRTHRIGHT ?

    GENESIS 25:32-33

    _____

2. WHO WAS JACOB TRICKED INTO MARRYING ?

    GENESIS 29:23-25

    _____

3. WHAT OLD TESTAMENT COUPLE HAD TWIN SONS ?

    GENESIS 25:20-24

    _____

4. WHOSE DAUGHTER DANCED AT HEROD'S BIRTHDAY PARTY ?

    MATTHEW 14:6

    _____

5. WHAT DID SOLOMON HAVE SEVEN HUNDRED OF ?

    1 KINGS 11:3

    _____

6. ON THE ROAD TO WHAT CITY DID THE GOOD SAMARITAN HELP THE BEATEN MAN ?

    LUKE 10:30-33

    _____

RACHEL

NEW YORK

ESAU

HERODIAS'

KIDS

ABRAHAM
      & SARAH

LEAH

ELIZABETH

REUBEN

WIVES

JERICHO

ISAAC
      & REBEKAH

MULTIPLE CHOICE
CIRCLE THE CORRECT ANSWER.

1. WHO WAS MOSES' WIFE?

   EXODUS 2:21

   A. HAGAR

   B. ZIPPORAH

   C. REBEKAH

2. WHO WAS THE FIRST PRIEST OF ISRAEL?

   EXODUS 28:3

   A. ABRAHAM

   B. MOSES

   C. AARON

3. WHO WAS A JUDGE FOR THE PEOPLE OF ISRAEL FOR TWENTY YEARS?

   JUDGES 16:31

   A. SAUL

   B. SAMSON

   C. DAVID

CONT'D NEXT PAGE...

...CONT'D FROM PREVIOUS PAGE.

4. WHO PREACHED IN THE WILDERNESS OF JUDEA?

MATTHEW 3:1

A. JOHN

B. JESUS

C. JOHN THE BAPTIST

5. WHAT WAS THE NAME OF MARY'S SISTER WHO WORKED HARD IN THE KITCHEN?

LUKE 10:40

A. RUTH

B. DEBORAH

C. MARTHA

6. WHO WROTE THE BOOK OF REVELATION?

REVELATION 1:4

A. PAUL

B. JOHN

C. PETER

MATCH THE ANSWERS

MATCH THE ANSWERS ON THE FOLLOWING
PAGE TO THE QUESTIONS BELOW.

1. HOW OLD WAS ABRAHAM WHEN ISAAC
   WAS BORN ?

   GENESIS 21:5

   _____

2. HOW MANY DAYS WAS SAUL BLIND ?

   ACTS 9:9

   _____

3. WHAT COMMANDMENT IS "HONOR YOUR
   FATHER AND YOUR MOTHER" ?

   EXODUS 20:12

   _____

4. WHAT DOES " GENESIS " MEAN ?

   _____

5. WHAT LANGUAGE WAS THE NEW
   TESTAMENT WRITTEN IN ?

   _____

6. WHAT NEW TESTAMENT BOOK TELLS
   OF JESUS GOING UP TO HEAVEN ?

   _____

END   EIGHTH

FOURTH   THREE

EIGHTY   BEGINNING

FIFTH   ONE HUNDRED

GREEK   ENGLISH

ACTS   JOHN

FILL IN THE BLANKS

WORD LIST

STAND	DOOR
KNOCK	ANYONE
VOICE	OPENS
EAT	HE

" HERE I AM! I _ _ _ _ _ AT THE _ _ _ _ AND _ _ _ _ _. IF _ _ _ _ _ _ HEARS MY _ _ _ _ _ AND _ _ _ _ _ THE DOOR, I WILL COME IN AND _ _ _ WITH HIM. AND _ _ WILL EAT WITH ME."

REVELATION 3:20

FILL IN THE BLANKS

WORD LIST

ASK	KNOCK
SEARCH	OPEN
FIND	GOD
YOU	DOOR

" CONTINUE TO _ _ _ AND _ _ _ _
WILL GIVE TO YOU . CONTINUE TO
_ _ _ _ _ _ AND _ _ _
WILL _ _ _ _ . CONTINUE TO
_ _ _ _ _ AND THE _ _ _ _
WILL BE _ _ _ _ FOR YOU ."

MATTHEW 7:7

29

MULTIPLE CHOICE

CIRCLE THE CORRECT ANSWER.

1. WHO WAS TAKEN OUT OF SODOM BEFORE IT WAS DESTROYED ?   GENESIS 19: 15-16

   A. ABRAHAM AND HIS FAMILY

   B. LOT AND HIS FAMILY

   C. ISAAC AND HIS FAMILY

2. WHO WAS ISAAC'S FATHER ?   GENESIS 21: 3

   A. JACOB

   B. NOAH

   C. ABRAHAM

3. WHO WAS SARAI'S MAID?   GENESIS 16:3

   A. REBEKAH

   B. HAGAR

   C. RUTH

CONT'D NEXT PAGE...

...CONT'D FROM PREVIOUS PAGE.

4. JESUS RAISED LAZARUS FROM THE DEAD. WHO WERE LAZARUS' SISTERS?

JOHN 11: 1-3

    A. MARY AND ELIZABETH

    B. RUTH AND NAOMI

    C. MARTHA AND MARY

5. WHAT DID JESUS SAY HE WOULD BUILD HIS CHURCH ON?

MATTHEW 16: 18

    A. THIS MOUNTAIN

    B. THIS HILL

    C. THIS ROCK

6. WHAT DID JUDAS DO AFTER HE BETRAYED JESUS?

MATTHEW 27: 5

    A. SAID SORRY

    B. CRIED

    C. HANGED HIMSELF

31

MULTIPLE CHOICE

CIRCLE THE CORRECT ANSWER.

1. WHAT DOES TESTAMENT MEAN?

    A. TO TEST

    B. AGREEMENT

    C. BOOKS

2. WHAT DID THE ISRAELITES PUT ON THEIR DOOR POSTS SO THAT THE DEATH ANGEL WOULD PASS BY?
   EXODUS 12:21:23

    A. GOAT'S BLOOD

    B. PAINT

    C. LAMB'S BLOOD

3. WHAT ARE WE TO POUR ON THE SICK SO THAT THE PRAYER OF FAITH WILL MAKE THEM WELL?
   JAMES 5:14

    A. MEDICINE

    B. WATER

    C. OIL

CONT'D NEXT PAGE...

4. WHAT ARE WE SUPPOSED TO DO WHEN
   WE SIN ?   JAMES 5:16

   A. FORGET ABOUT IT

   B. CONFESS IT TO EACH OTHER

   C. PRETEND IT DIDN'T HAPPEN

5. JESUS CALLED MATTHEW TO BE A DISCIPLE.
   WHAT WAS HE BEFORE JESUS CALLED HIM ?

   A. A FISHERMAN   MATTHEW 9:9

   B. A TAX COLLECTOR

   C. A BASEBALL PLAYER

6. WHAT DID JESUS SAY HE WOULD MAKE
   PETER AND ANDREW ?   MARK 1:16-17

   A. SINGERS

   B. KINGS

   C. FISHERS OF MEN

MATCH THE ANSWERS

MATCH THE ANSWERS ON THE FOLLOWING PAGE TO THE QUESTIONS BELOW.

1. IN THE ARMOR OF GOD, WHAT IS THE SHIELD CALLED?   EPHESIANS 6:16

   _____

2. WHAT IS THE HELMET CALLED?
                                   EPHESIANS 6:17

   _____

3. WHAT IS THE SWORD CALLED?
                                   EPHESIANS 6:17

   _____

4. WHAT IS THE BELT CALLED?
                                   EPHESIANS 6:14

   _____

5. WHAT INGREDIENT IN THE KITCHEN DID JESUS SAY WE WERE LIKE?
                                   MATTHEW 5:13

   _____

6. WHAT BOOK OF THE BIBLE HAS THE MOST CHAPTERS?

   _____

SALVATION   PROTECTION

WORD OF GOD   SPIRIT

FAITH   DOUBT

SUGAR   TRUTH

HALF TRUTH   SALT

PROVERBS   PSALMS

MATCH THE ANSWERS

MATCH THE ANSWERS ON THE FOLLOWING
PAGE TO THE QUESTIONS BELOW.

1. IN THE DESERT, GOD GAVE THE ISRAELITES
   MANNA TO EAT. WHAT ELSE DID GOD GIVE
   THEM?

   EXODUS 16:13

   _____

2. WHAT DOES JESUS GIVE TO THOSE WHO
   CHOOSE TO FOLLOW HIM?

   JOHN 10:27-28

   _____

3. WHAT SPECIAL DAY WAS IT WHEN THE
   BELIEVERS RECEIVED THE HOLY SPIRIT?

   ACTS 2:1-4

   _____

4. A MAN REAPS WHAT HE ... WHAT?

   GALATIANS 6:7

   _____

5. WHAT DID JESUS SAY HE HAD OVERCOME?

   JOHN 16:33

   _____

6. IN WHAT COUNTRY DID ISAAC FIND
   A WIFE?

   GENESIS 24:4,10

   _____

ETERNAL LIFE	EARTH
QUAILS	CHICKEN
EASTER	CANDY
EATS	PENTECOST
WORLD	SOWS
MAGOG	MESOPOTAMIA

FILL IN THE BLANKS

" _ _ _ _ _ SAID, ' A

_ _ _ _ _ _ DOES NOT

_ _ _ _ ONLY BY _ _ _ _ _ _

_ _ _ _ _ _ . BUT A PERSON

LIVES _ _ _ _ _ _ _ _ _ _ _

THE _ _ _ _ SAYS. ' "

MATTHEW 4:4

38

FILL IN THE BLANKS

WORD LIST

BEGINS   RESPECT

WISDOM   LORD

KNOWLEDGE   FOOLISH

SELF-CONTROL

"_ _ _ _ _ _ _ _

_ _ _ _ _ _ WITH

_ _ _ _ _ _ _ FOR THE

_ _ _ _ . BUT _ _ _ _ _ _ _

PEOPLE HATE _ _ _ _ _ _ AND

_ _ _ _ - _ _ _ _ _ _ ."

PROVERBS 1:7

FILL IN THE BLANKS

WORD LIST

LOVE   KINDNESS

JOY   FAITHFULNESS

SELF-CONTROL PEACE

GENTLENESS   PATIENCE

GOODNESS

" BUT THE SPIRIT GIVES _ _ _ _ _ ,

_ _ _ , _ _ _ _ _ ,

_ _ _ _ _ _ _ ,

_ _ _ _ _ _ _ _ ,

_ _ _ _ _ _ _ ,

_ _ _ _ _ _ _ _ _

_ _ _ _ _ _ _ _ _ ,

AND _ _ _ _ _ -

_ _ _ _ _ _ _ . THERE IS

NO LAW THAT SAYS THESE THINGS

ARE WRONG . "

GALATIANS 5 : 22-23

FILL IN THE BLANKS

WORD LIST

HELPER   EVERYTHING

NAME   YOU

HOLY   REMEMBER

FATHER   HE

" BUT THE _ _ _ _ _ _ WILL
TEACH YOU _ _ _ _ _ _ _ _ _ _.
_ _ WILL CAUSE YOU TO
_ _ _ _ _ _ _ _ ALL THE
THINGS I TOLD _ _ _. THIS
HELPER IS THE _ _ _ _ SPIRIT
WHOM THE _ _ _ _ _ _ WILL
SEND IN MY _ _ _ _."

JOHN 14:26

41

MATCH THE ANSWERS

MATCH THE ANSWERS ON THE FOLLOWING PAGE TO THE QUESTIONS BELOW.

1. IN THE PARABLE OF THE TALENTS, HOW MANY SERVANTS WERE GIVEN TALENTS?

   _____   MATTHEW 25:14-15

2. HOW OLD WAS JAIRUS' DAUGHTER WHEN SHE GOT SICK?   LUKE 8:42

   _____

3. HOW MANY WARNINGS, OR "WOES", DID JESUS GIVE TO THE PHARISEES?

   _____   MATTHEW 23:13-36

4. HOW MANY WIVES DID JACOB HAVE?

                                      GENESIS 29:24-30
   _____   30:4,9

5. HOW MANY PIECES OF SILVER WAS JUDAS PAID TO BETRAY JESUS?

                                      MATTHEW 26:15
   _____

6. HOW MANY CONCUBINES DID KING SOLOMON HAVE?   1 KINGS 11:3

   _____

NINE	EIGHT
FOUR	THREE
TWELVE	TEN
FIVE	SEVEN
THIRTY	ONE HUNDRED
ONE THOUSAND	THREE HUNDRED

MATCH THE ANSWERS

MATCH THE ANSWERS ON THE FOLLOWING PAGE TO THE QUESTIONS BELOW.

1. HOW MANY WERE AT THE LAST SUPPER WITH JESUS?

   MATTHEW 26: 19-20

   _____

2. HOW LONG IS A MILLENIUM?

   REVELATION 20: 4, 6-7

   _____

3. WHICH OLD TESTAMENT BOOK TELLS ABOUT THE LIFE OF ABRAHAM?

   _____

4. WHAT PEOPLE WANTED TO KNOW THE SECRET OF SAMSON'S STRENGTH?

   JUDGES 16: 4-5

   _____

5. WHO WAS THE ONLY FEMALE JUDGE OF ISRAEL?

   JUDGES 4: 4-14

   _____

6. THE LORD SAID HE IS THE ALPHA AND THE OMEGA. WHAT DOES OMEGA MEAN?

   REVELATION 22: 13

   _____

TEN THOUSAND YEARS	PHILISTINES
EXODUS	ISRAELITES
ELEVEN	TWELVE
RUTH	LAST, END
FIRST, BEGINNING	DEBORAH
GENESIS	ONE THOUSAND YEARS

45

MULTIPLE CHOICE

CIRCLE THE CORRECT ANSWER.

1. WHO WAS JOSEPH'S MOTHER?

   GENESIS 30:22-24

   A. LEAH

   B. RACHEL

   C. REBEKAH

2. WHO WAS THE FIRST KING OF ISRAEL?

   1 SAMUEL 10:21-25

   A. AARON

   B. DAVID

   C. SAUL

3. WHAT WAS BELTESHAZZAR'S OTHER NAME?

   DANIEL 1:7

   A. SIMON

   B. DANIEL

   C. JOB

CONT'D NEXT PAGE...

4. WHO WAS THE COUSIN OF MORDECAI
THAT BECAME A QUEEN? ESTHER 2:15-17

      A. RUTH

      B. NAOMI

      C. ESTHER

5. WHO WROTE THE RIDDLE ABOUT
THE LION? JUDGES 14:16-18

      A. JUDGES

      B. SOLOMON

      C. SAMSON

6. WHO CALLED DOWN FIRE FROM
HEAVEN? 2 KINGS 1:10

      A. ELISHA

      B. ELIJAH

      C. JEREMIAH

MULTIPLE CHOICE
CIRCLE THE CORRECT ANSWER.

1. WHAT EXCUSE DID MOSES GIVE TO GOD FOR WHY HE DIDN'T WANT TO GO TO EGYPT?

   A. "I'M TOO TIRED." EXODUS 4:10-16

   B. "I MADE OTHER PLANS."

   C. "I AM SLOW TO SPEAK."

2. WHAT DID JOSEPH INTERPRET FOR PHARAOH?

   GENESIS 41:14-36

   A. HIS WIFE'S DREAMS

   B. A RECIPE FOR PUDDING

   C. HIS DREAMS

3. JESUS SAID THAT WHEN HE RETURNS AGAIN, HE WILL COME LIKE A...WHAT?

   REVELATION 16:15

   A. FLASH OF LIGHTNING

   B. BOLT OF THUNDER

   C. THIEF IN THE NIGHT

CONT'D NEXT PAGE...

...CONT'D FROM PREVIOUS PAGE.

4. WHAT DID THE WOMEN BRING TO JESUS' TOMB?

MARK 16:1

    A. FLOWERS

    B. SWEET SPICES

    C. PEOPLE

5. WHAT DID ESAU DO FOR A LIVING?

GENESIS 25:27

    A. FARM

    B. BUILD

    C. HUNT

6. IN THE PARABLE OF THE SOWER, WHAT DOES THE SEED STAND FOR?

LUKE 8:11

    A. A PLANT

    B. CORN

    C. THE WORD OF GOD

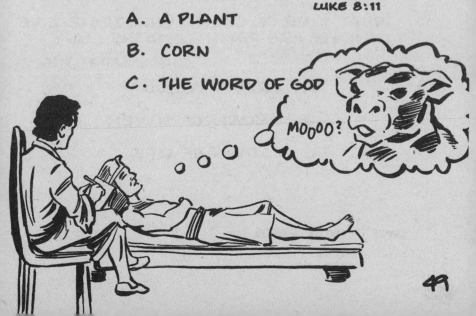

MULTIPLE CHOICE

CIRCLE THE CORRECT ANSWER.

1. WHAT DID JESUS TELL THE DISCIPLES TO DO IF THEY WERE NOT WELCOME AT SOMEONE'S HOME?

   MATTHEW 10:14

   A. GET ANGRY.

   B. WHINE AND CRY.

   C. SHAKE THE DUST OFF YOUR FEET.

2. WHAT WAS JOHN THE BAPTIST'S CLOTHING MADE OF?

   MATTHEW 3:4

   A. SILK

   B. WOOL

   C. CAMEL'S HAIR

3. WHAT KIND OF CROWN WILL JESUS GIVE US IF WE ARE FAITHFUL TO THE END?

   REVELATION 2:10

   A. CROWN OF GOLD

   B. CROWN OF SILVER

   C. CROWN OF LIFE

CONT'D NEXT PAGE...

4. WHAT ARE WE TOLD TO TAKE UP TO
   FOLLOW JESUS?   MATTHEW 10:38

   A. OUR SUITCASES

   B. OUR CROSSES

   C. OUR COATS

5. FAITH WITHOUT WHAT IS DEAD?
                                   JAMES 2:20

   A. WORDS

   B. WORKS

   C. WISDOM

6. WHAT DID DANIEL AND HIS FRIENDS
   REFUSE TO EAT AND DRINK AT THE
   KING'S TABLE?
                                   DANIEL 1:8

   A. LIVER, ONIONS, AND
      CARROT JUICE

   B. MEAT AND WINE

   C. PIZZA AND SODA

FILL IN THE BLANKS

" _ _ _ _ _ IN THE _ _ _ _ WITH ALL YOUR _ _ _ _ _ . DON'T _ _ _ _ _ _ ON YOUR _ _ _ UNDERSTANDING. _ _ _ _ _ _ _ THE LORD IN _ _ _ _ _ _ _ _ _ _ YOU DO. AND HE WILL GIVE YOU _ _ _ _ _ _ _ ! "

PROVERBS 3:5-6

52

FILL IN THE BLANKS

" _ _ _ _ _ _ ON THE _ _ _ _.

TRUST HIM AND _ _ WILL TAKE

_ _ _ _ OF YOU. THEN YOUR

_ _ _ _ _ _ _ _ WILL

SHINE LIKE THE _ _ _. YOUR

_ _ _ _ _ _ _ WILL SHINE

LIKE THE _ _ _ _ _ _ SUN."

PSALM 37:5-6

S3

FILL IN THE BLANKS

" _ _ _ _ AND _ _ _ _ _
THE _ _ _ _ _ . DON'T BE
_ _ _ _ _ _ WHEN OTHERS
GET _ _ _ _ _ OR WHEN
SOMEONE ELSE'S PLANS SUCCEED.
DON'T GET _ _ _ _ _ _ . DON'T
BE UPSET; IT ONLY _ _ _ _ _
TO _ _ _ _ _ _ _ . "

PSALM 37:7-8

FILL IN THE BLANKS

" _ _ _ _ _ _ _ YOURSELVES

AND BE _ _ _ _ _ _ _.

THE _ _ _ _ _ IS YOUR

_ _ _ _ _. AND _ _ GOES

AROUND LIKE A _ _ _ _ _ _ _

LION _ _ _ _ _ _ _ FOR

SOMEONE TO _ _ _."

1 PETER 5:8

YUM!
— YUM!

55

MATCH THE ANSWERS

MATCH THE ANSWERS ON THE FOLLOWING PAGE TO THE QUESTIONS BELOW.

1. WHO DID ISAAC BLESS INSTEAD OF ESAU?
   GENESIS 27:21-23

   _____

2. WHO TOLD THE BROTHERS OF JOSEPH NOT TO HARM JOSEPH?
   GENESIS 37:22

   _____

3. WHO SAID THEY SHOULD SELL JOSEPH RATHER THAN KILL HIM?
   GENESIS 37:26-27

   _____

4. WHO HAD A DREAM ABOUT THE SUN, MOON, AND STARS BOWING DOWN TO HIM?
   GENESIS 37:5-9

   _____

5. WHO PURCHASED JOSEPH AS A SLAVE?
   GENESIS 37:36

   _____

6. WHO WAS JOSEPH'S MOTHER?
   GENESIS 30:22-24

   _____

LEAH	RACHEL
BENJAMIN	JACOB
JUDAH	REUBEN
PONTIUS PILATE	POTIPHAR
SAMSON	JOSEPH
ZIPPORAH	JOB

MATCH THE ANSWERS

MATCH THE ANSWERS ON THE FOLLOWING PAGE TO THE QUESTIONS BELOW.

1. WHO WAS THE FATHER OF JAMES AND JOHN?

   LUKE 5:10

   _____

2. WHAT TWO DISCIPLES FOLLOWED JESUS FIRST?

   MATTHEW 4:18

   _____

3. HOW MANY BOOKS IN THE NEW TESTAMENT HAVE ONLY ONE CHAPTER?

   _____

4. THE FOUR GOSPELS ARE ABOUT WHOM?

   _____

5. WHAT DO WE CALL THE DAY IN WHICH WE REMEMBER JESUS' DEATH ON THE CROSS?

   _____

6. WHICH DISCIPLE WAS SENT TO THE ISLAND OF PATMOS?

   REVELATION 1:9

   _____

ANSWERS TO THE PREVIOUS PAGE.

FOUR	JOHN
JOHN THE BAPTIST	MATTHEW & JOHN
EASTER	ZEBEDEE
ZECHARIAH	THREE
PAUL	JESUS
GOOD FRIDAY	SIMON PETER & ANDREW

MULTIPLE CHOICE

CIRCLE THE CORRECT ANSWER.

1. ON WHAT WAS JOHN THE BAPTIST'S HEAD PUT TO GIVE TO HERODIAS' DAUGHTER?

   MATTHEW 14:8

   A. STICK

   B. PLATTER

   C. BOWL

2. WHAT HAPPENED TO THE MEN THAT THREW SHADRACH, MESHACH, AND ABEDNEGO INTO THE FIERY FURNACE?

   DANIEL 3:22

   A. THEIR HAIR WAS SINGED.

   B. THE HEAT OF THE FIRE KILLED THEM.

   C. THEY GOT VERY WARM.

3. WHAT DOES JAMES SAY SHALL SAVE THE SICK?

   JAMES 5:15

   A. A DOCTOR

   B. GOING TO THE HOSPITAL

   C. A PRAYER OF FAITH

CONT'D NEXT PAGE...

4. WHAT WAS JOHN THE BAPTIST UNWORTHY
   TO UNTIE?

   MARK 1:7

   A. JESUS' NECKTIE

   B. JESUS' CLOAK

   C. JESUS' SANDALS

5. WHY DID MARY AND JOSEPH GO TO
   BETHLEHEM?

   LUKE 2:1-4

   A. FOR A VACATION

   B. TO REGISTER THEIR
      NAMES TO PAY TAXES

   C. TO VISIT ELIZABETH

6. WHAT HAPPENED TO THE WATERS OF
   MARAH WHEN MOSES THREW A TREE IN?

   EXODUS 15:23-25

   A. THE TREE BLOCKED THE WATER.

   B. MADE THE WATER SWEET
      OR GOOD TO DRINK

   C. MADE A MESS

MULTIPLE CHOICE
CIRCLE THE CORRECT ANSWER.

1. WHAT WAS GIVEN TO PAUL TO KEEP HIM HUMBLE?

   2 CORINTHIANS 12:7

   A. A THORN IN THE FLESH

   B. BLINDNESS

   C. POVERTY

2. FOR WHAT DID ESAU SELL HIS BIRTHRIGHT?

   GENESIS 25:34

   A. HAMBURGER AND FRIES

   B. A BOWL OF STEW

   C. A NEW SUIT OF CLOTHES

3. WHAT DID JESUS SAY THE RICH MAN MUST SELL TO HAVE TREASURES IN HEAVEN?

   MATTHEW 19:21

   A. HIS HOUSE

   B. ALL HIS POSSESSIONS

   C. HIS BROTHER

CONT'D NEXT PAGE...

4. WHAT WAS FOUND IN BENJAMIN'S
   PACK ?
   GENESIS 44:12

   A. A FROG

   B. HIS CLOTHES

   C. JOSEPH'S SILVER CUP

5. WHAT KIND OF TREE DID JESUS
   CONDEMN ?
   MATTHEW 21:19

   A. AN APPLE TREE

   B. A FIG TREE

   C. A PLUM TREE

6. WHAT PARABLE TELLS OF THE SON THAT
   LEAVES HOME AND WASTES ALL HIS
   MONEY ?
   LUKE 15:11-32

   A. THE STUBBORN SON

   B. THE FIRST SON

   C. THE PRODIGAL SON

FILL IN THE BLANKS

" MOST IMPORTANTLY, _ _ _ _
EACH OTHER _ _ _ _ _ _ _ .
LOVE HAS A WAY OF NOT
_ _ _ _ _ _ _ AT _ _ _ _ _ _
SINS. _ _ _ _ _ YOUR
_ _ _ _ _ _ TO _ _ _ _ _
OTHER WITHOUT
_ _ _ _ _ _ _ _ _ _ _ . "

1 PETER 4: 8-9

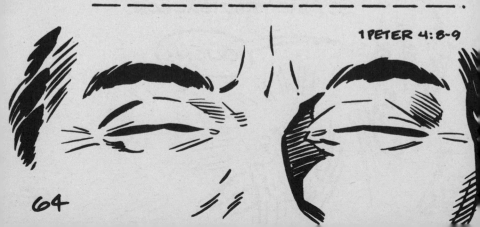

FILL IN THE BLANKS

WORD LIST

GIFT	GRACE
DIFFERENT	RESPONSIBLE
SERVANTS	YOU
GOD'S	EACH

" _____ OF YOU RECEIVED A

SPIRITUAL _____ . GOD HAS

SHOWN YOU HIS _____

IN GIVING YOU _____

GIFTS. AND ___ ARE LIKE

_____ WHO ARE

_____

FOR USING _____ GIFTS."

1 PETER 4:10

65

READ 2 PETER 1:5-7. WHAT SHOULD YOU ADD TO EACH QUALITY BELOW?

LOOK ON THE FOLLOWING PAGE FOR YOUR ANSWERS.

FAITH

_____

GOODNESS

_____

KNOWLEDGE

_____

SELF-CONTROL

_____

ABILITY TO HOLD ON

_____

SERVICE TO GOD

_____

BROTHERLY KINDNESS

_____

THIS SCRIPTURE CONTINUES IN VERSES 8-9:

" IF ALL THESE THINGS ARE IN YOU AND ARE GROWING, THEY WILL HELP YOU NEVER TO BE USELESS. THEY WILL HELP YOUR KNOWLEDGE OF OUR LORD JESUS CHRIST AND MAKE YOUR LIVES BETTER. BUT IF ANYONE DOES NOT HAVE THESE THINGS, HE CANNOT SEE CLEARLY. HE IS BLIND. HE HAS FORGOTTEN THAT HE WAS MADE CLEAN FROM HIS PAST SINS. "

WHAT A GREAT PROMISE!

KNOWLEDGE

ABILITY TO HOLD ON

LOVE

GOODNESS

SERVICE TO GOD

BROTHERLY KINDNESS

SELF - CONTROL

MATCH THE COLUMNS

WHO WAS WHOSE WIFE?

DRAW A LINE TO MATCH HUSBAND TO WIFE.

ABRAHAM

BOAZ

DAVID

KING XERXES

ELKANAH

HEROD

AQUILA

RUTH
RUTH 4:13

PRISCILLA
ACTS 18:2

HERODIAS
MARK 6:17

BATHSHEBA
2 SAMUEL 12: 12: 24

ESTHER
ESTHER 2:16-17

HANNAH
1 SAMUEL 1: 1-2

SARAH
GENESIS 17:15

TRUE / FALSE

1. JOSEPH WAS TWENTY-THREE YEARS OLD WHEN HIS BROTHERS SOLD HIM TO THE ISHMAELITES.

   GENESIS 37:2   TRUE ____ FALSE ____

2. LAZARUS HAD BEEN DEAD FOR THREE DAYS WHEN JESUS CALLED HIM OUT OF HIS TOMB, RAISING HIM TO LIFE.

   JOHN 11:39   TRUE ____ FALSE ____

3. MOSES AND ABRAHAM APPEARED WITH JESUS ON THE MOUNT OF TRANSFIGURATION.

   MATTHEW 17:3   TRUE ____ FALSE ____

4. JESUS FED FOUR THOUSAND PEOPLE WITH A FEW LOAVES OF BREAD AND SOME FISH.

   MATTHEW 15:29-38 TRUE ____ FALSE ____

69

MULTIPLE CHOICE

CIRCLE THE CORRECT ANSWER.

1. HE WANTED TO PUT HIS HAND IN JESUS' SIDE AFTER THE RESURRECTION. JOHN 20:24-25

   A. THOMAS

   B. JOHN

   C. PETER

2. JESUS CALLED HIM AWAY FROM HIS JOB AS A TAX COLLECTOR. MATTHEW 9:9

   A. PHILIP

   B. MATTHEW

   C. JAMES

3. JESUS HEALED HIS MOTHER-IN-LAW. MATTHEW 8:14-15

   A. JOHN

   B. JAMES

   C. PETER

CONT'D NEXT PAGE...

... CONT'D FROM PREVIOUS PAGE.

4. HE GAVE JESUS A KISS, BUT NOT OUT
   OF LOVE.
   LUKE 22:47

   A. PONTIUS PILATE

   B. JUDAS ISCARIOT

   C. JOHN

5. HE BAPTIZED AN ETHIOPIAN HE MET
   ON THE ROAD.
   ACTS 8:27-38

   A. PHILIP

   B. SIMON

   C. ANDREW

6. HE AND HIS BROTHER LEFT THEIR
   FATHER TO FOLLOW JESUS.
   MATTHEW 4:18

   A. PETER

   B. THOMAS

   C. JUDAS

FINISH THE VERSE

HERE ARE SOME OF THE BEATITUDES.
FINISH THEM BY MATCHING THEM WITH
THE PHRASES ON THE FOLLOWING PAGE.

1. "BLESSED ARE THE POOR IN SPIRIT."

_____

2. "BLESSED ARE THOSE WHO MOURN."

_____

3. "BLESSED ARE THE MEEK."

_____

4. "BLESSED ARE THOSE WHO HUNGER AND
THIRST FOR RIGHTEOUSNESS."

_____

5. "BLESSED ARE THE MERCIFUL."

_____

6. "BLESSED ARE THE PEACEMAKERS."

_____

MATTHEW 5:1-10
(NEW INTERNATIONAL VERSION)

" THEY WILL BE COMFORTED."

" THEY WILL BE SHOWN MERCY."

" THEY WILL INHERIT THE EARTH."

" THEY WILL BE WITH GOD. "

" THEY WILL BE CALLED SONS OF GOD. "

" THEIRS IS THE KINGDOM OF HEAVEN."

" THEY WILL BE FILLED."

MATCH THE SAYING

MATCH THE SAYING BELOW WITH THE
PERSON WHO SAID IT FROM THE
FOLLOWING PAGE.

1. " YOUR FATHER AND I WERE VERY
WORRIED ABOUT YOU. WE HAVE BEEN
LOOKING FOR YOU. "

LUKE 2:48

_____

2. " I SINNED. I GAVE YOU AN
INNOCENT MAN TO BE KILLED. "

MATTHEW 27:4

_____

3. " AS FOR ME AND MY FAMILY, WE WILL
SERVE THE LORD. "

JOSHUA 24:14-15

_____

4. " NO! I WANT CAESAR TO HEAR MY
CASE! "

ACTS 25:10-11

_____

5. " I HAVE SINNED AGAINST THE
LORD. "

2 SAMUEL 12:13

_____

JUDAS JOSHUA

JESUS MARY, HIS MOTHER

PAUL MOSES

JOSEPH JUDAS ISCARIOT

DAVID JOHN THE
 BAPTIST

FILL IN THE BLANKS

WORD LIST

ANSWER	MORNING
GOD	CRY
WAIT	YOU
NEED	VOICE

"LISTEN TO MY _ _ _ FOR

HELP. MY KING AND MY _ _ _

I PRAY TO _ _ _. LORD,

EVERY _ _ _ _ _ _ _ YOU

HEAR MY _ _ _ _ _ _.

EVERY MORNING I TELL YOU

WHAT I _ _ _ _ _. AND

I _ _ _ _ FOR YOUR

_ _ _ _ _ _."

PSALM 5:2-3

FILL IN THE BLANKS

WORD LIST

TIRED   WORK

HEAVY   SOULS

REST   EASY

LOADS   LEARN

" COME TO ME, ALL OF YOU WHO
ARE _ _ _ _ _ _ AND HAVE
HEAVY _ _ _ _ _ _. I WILL
GIVE YOU _ _ _ _. ACCEPT
MY _ _ _ _ AND _ _ _ _ _
FROM ME. I AM GENTLE AND
HUMBLE IN SPIRIT. AND YOU
WILL FIND REST FOR YOUR
_ _ _ _ _ _. THE WORK I
ASK YOU TO ACCEPT IS
_ _ _ _. THE LOAD I
GIVE YOU TO CARRY IS NOT
_ _ _ _ _. "

MATTHEW 11: 28-30

77

MULTIPLE CHOICE

CIRCLE THE CORRECT ANSWER.

1. HOW MANY TIMES DID JOSEPH AND MARY RUN FOR THEIR LIVES WITH JESUS?

   MATTHEW 2:14-21

   A. ONCE

   B. TWICE

   C. THREE TIMES

2. HOW MANY DAYS DID GOD GIVE THE PEOPLE OF NINEVEH TO TURN FROM THEIR SIN OR THEY WOULD BE DESTROYED?

   JONAH 3:4

   A. SEVEN DAYS

   B. FORTY DAYS

   C. TWENTY DAYS

3. HOW LONG DID IT GO ON WITHOUT RAINING AFTER ELIJAH PRAYED?

   LUKE 4:25

   A. TWO AND A HALF DAYS

   B. THREE AND A HALF DAYS

   C. THREE AND A HALF YEARS

CONT'D NEXT PAGE...

... CONT'D FROM PREVIOUS PAGE.

4. HOW MANY PEOPLE DID KING NEBUCHADNEZZAR SEE WALKING IN THE FURNACE?

DANIEL 3:25

    A. THREE

    B. FOUR

    C. FIVE

5. HOW MANY BROTHERS DID JESUS HAVE?

MARK 6:3

    A. NONE

    B. TWO

    C. FOUR

6. WHICH PLAGUE ON EGYPT INVOLVED HAIL AND FIRE?

EXODUS 9:22-25

    A. THE THIRD

    B. THE FIFTH

    C. THE SEVENTH

MULTIPLE CHOICE

CIRCLE THE CORRECT ANSWER.

1. HOW OLD WAS JESUS WHEN HE WAS BAPTIZED AND STARTED HIS MINISTRY?

   LUKE 3:21-23

   A. ABOUT NINETEEN

   B. ABOUT TWENTY-FIVE

   C. ABOUT THIRTY

2. HOW LONG WAS MOSES ON THE MOUNTAIN TO RECEIVE THE TEN COMMANDMENTS?

   EXODUS 24:18

   A. OVERNIGHT

   B. FORTY DAYS

   C. FORTY DAYS AND NIGHTS

3. WHEN HE WAS PRAYING, HOW MANY TIMES DID JESUS WAKE HIS DISCIPLES IN THE GARDEN OF GETHSEMANE?

   MATTHEW 26:39-45

   A. ONCE

   B. TWICE

   C. THREE TIMES

CONT'D NEXT PAGE...

4. WHAT PIECE OF CLOTHING DID THE SOLDIERS MAKE JESUS WEAR?

JOHN 19:2-5

    A. A WHITE ROBE

    B. A PURPLE ROBE

    C. A BLUE ROBE

5. WHAT WOMAN LED AN ARMY INTO BATTLE?

JUDGES 4:6-9

    A. RUTH

    B. DEBORAH

    C. ESTHER

6. WHAT OTHER NAME WERE THE WISE MEN CALLED?

MATTHEW 2:1

    A. SMART MEN

    B. KINGS

    C. MAGI

MATCH THE ANSWERS

MATCH THE ANSWERS ON THE FOLLOWING PAGE TO THE QUESTIONS BELOW.

1. ON HIS THIRD MISSIONARY JOURNEY, WHERE WAS PAUL ARRESTED?

   ACTS 21: 15-36

   _____

2. HOW MANY BASKETS OF BREAD WERE LEFT AFTER JESUS FED THE FOUR THOUSAND?

   MATTHEW 15: 34-37

   _____

3. WHO BROUGHT DORCAS, A DISCIPLE IN JOPPA, BACK TO LIFE?

   ACTS 9: 39-41

   _____

4. WHO DID KING DAVID SEND TO THE FRONT LINE SO THAT HE WOULD BE KILLED IN BATTLE?

   2 SAMUEL 11: 14-17

   _____

5. WHO WANTED JESUS' TOMB SEALED AND GUARDED SO NO ONE COULD STEAL THE BODY?

   MATTHEW 27: 62-64

   _____

6. WHO THREATENED TO KILL ALL THE BELIEVERS OF JESUS?

   ACTS 9: 1

   _____

PAUL

PRIESTS

TWELVE BASKETS

ABSALOM

SAUL

JERUSALEM

SEVEN BASKETS

ROME

PHARISEES

PETER

URIAH

PONTIUS
PILATE

TRUE / FALSE

1. THE BOOK OF EXODUS RECORDS THAT JOSEPH DIED WHEN HE WAS ONE HUNDRED AND TEN YEARS OLD.

   GENESIS 50:26   TRUE ____ FALSE ____

2. MOSES WAS ABRAHAM'S FATHER.

   GENESIS 11:27   TRUE ____ FALSE ____

3. HAM, THE SON OF NOAH, HAD FOUR SONS.

   GENESIS 10:6   TRUE ____ FALSE ____

4. PONTIUS PILATE ORDERED THREE SOLDIERS TO GUARD JESUS' TOMB.

   MATTHEW 27:65   TRUE ____ FALSE ____

5. JONATHAN WAS SAMUEL'S SON.

TRUE / FALSE

1. JESUS WAS BORN IN JERUSALEM.
   MATTHEW 2:12   TRUE ____ FALSE ____

2. THE THREE WISE MEN RETURNED
   TO KING HEROD WITH INFORMATION
   ABOUT JESUS.
   MATTHEW 2:27   TRUE ____ FALSE ____

3. JESUS WAS CALLED A NAZARENE
   BECAUSE HE LIVED IN THE TOWN OF
   NAZARETH.
   MATTHEW 2:23   TRUE ____ FALSE ____

4. PETER BETRAYED JESUS AS THE LORD
   HAD SAID HE WOULD.
   JOHN 13:26   TRUE ____ FALSE ____

5. GOLIATH WAS AN ISRAELITE AND A
   FRIEND OF THE YOUNG DAVID.
   1 SAMUEL 17:4   TRUE ____ FALSE ____

TRUE / FALSE

1. KING SAUL WANTED TO KILL DAVID BECAUSE OF HIS JEALOUSY.

   1 SAMUEL 19:1

   TRUE ____ FALSE ____

2. NOAH LIVED FOR NINE HUNDRED AND THIRTY-FIVE YEARS.

   GENESIS 9:29

   TRUE ____ FALSE ____

3. AT FIRST, JOSEPH FELT HE SHOULD DIVORCE MARY WHEN HE FOUND OUT SHE WAS PREGNANT.

   MATTHEW 1:19

   TRUE ____ FALSE ____

4. JESUS' FATHER, JOSEPH, WAS A SON OF DAVID.

   MATTHEW 1:20

   TRUE ____ FALSE ____

5. EMMANUEL MEANS "GOD WITH US" AND IS ANOTHER NAME FOR JESUS FROM THE OLD TESTAMENT.

   MATTHEW 1:23
   ISAIAH 7:14

   TRUE ____ FALSE ____

MATCH THE SAYING

MATCH THE SAYING BELOW WITH THE
PERSON WHO SAID IT FROM THE
FOLLOWING PAGE.

1. " THIS PUNISHMENT IS MORE THAN
   I CAN STAND ! "   GENESIS 4:13

   _____

2. " THERE IS ONLY ONE GOD. AND THERE
   IS ONLY ONE WAY THAT PEOPLE CAN
   REACH GOD. "   1 TIMOTHY 1:1
                                           2:5

   _____

3. " BUT THE MOST HIGH DOES NOT LIVE IN
   HOUSES THAT MEN BUILD WITH THEIR HANDS."
                                        ACTS 6:8
                                            7:48

   _____

4. " SEE, TODAY I AM LETTING YOU CHOOSE A
   BLESSING OR A CURSE. "
                                 DEUTERONOMY 5:1
                                           11:26

   _____

5. " AS SURELY AS THE LORD LIVES, DAVID
   WON'T BE PUT TO DEATH. "
                                  1 SAMUEL 19:6

   _____

TIMOTHY   NEHEMIAH

STEPHEN   MOSES

ISAIAH   CAIN

SAUL   JOB

JONATHAN   PAUL

"...DAVID WON'T BE PUT TO DEATH!"

AT LEAST NOT TODAY...

88

TRUE / FALSE

1. LOT WAS THE SON OF ABRAHAM.
   GENESIS 11:31
   TRUE _____ FALSE _____

2. SAUL WAS NOT JONATHAN'S FATHER.
   HE WAS DAVID'S FATHER.
   1 SAMUEL 19:1
   TRUE _____ FALSE _____

3. JONATHAN DID NOT LIKE DAVID AND
   WANTED NOTHING TO DO WITH HIM.
   1 SAMUEL 19:2
   TRUE _____ FALSE _____

4. SHEM, NOAH'S SON, HAD AN OLDER
   BROTHER NAMED JAPHETH.
   GENESIS 10:21
   TRUE _____ FALSE _____

5. MARY WAS PLEDGED, OR BETROTHED,
   TO MARRY JOSEPH.
   MATTHEW 1:18
   TRUE _____ FALSE _____

MULTIPLE CHOICE
CIRCLE THE CORRECT ANSWER.

1. WHO WAS JACOB'S FIRST SON?

   GENESIS 46:8

   A. ESAU

   B. REUBEN

   C. ISAAC

2. HOW MANY SONS DID TERAH HAVE?

   GENESIS 11:26

   A. ONE

   B. TWO

   C. THREE

3. WHAT WAS NIMROD KNOWN AS?

   GENESIS 10:9

   A. A GREAT WARRIOR

   B. A GREAT FARMER

   C. A GREAT HUNTER

CONT'D NEXT PAGE ...

4. WHAT WAS THE NAME OF SAMUEL'S FIRSTBORN SON?

1 SAMUEL 8:2

    A. ABIJAH

    B. JOEL

    C. SAMUEL, JR.

5. HOW DID PETER ESCAPE FROM PRISON?

ACTS 12:7-10

    A. HE DRILLED HIS WAY OUT.

    B. HIS FRIENDS HID A FILE IN A CAKE.

    C. AN ANGEL OF THE LORD GOT HIM OUT.

6. WHAT IS ONE OF THE FOUR LIVING CREATURES IN THE VISION OF HEAVEN?

REVELATION 4:7

    A. A CAT

    B. AN EAGLE

    C. A BUDGIE

MULTIPLE CHOICE

CIRCLE THE CORRECT ANSWER.

1. WHO WROTE THE BOOK OF EPHESIANS IN THE NEW TESTAMENT ?

   EPHESIANS 1:1

   A. EPHESIA

   B. TIMOTHY

   C. PAUL

2. HOW MANY LOAVES OF BREAD AND FISH DID JESUS USE TO FEED THE FOUR THOUSAND ?

   MATTHEW 15:34

   A. THREE LOAVES OF BREAD AND SEVEN FISH

   B. SEVEN LOAVES OF BREAD AND A FEW FISH

   C. FOUR THOUSAND LOAVES OF BREAD AND FOUR THOUSAND FISH

3. THE SECOND PLAGUE ON EGYPT WAS..?

   EXODUS 8:1-15

   A. FROGS

   B. LOCUSTS

   C. FLIES

 CONT'D NEXT PAGE...

... CONT'D FROM PREVIOUS PAGE.

4. HOW DID SAUL KILL HIMSELF?

1 SAMUEL 31:4

    A. HUNG HIMSELF

    B. FELL ON A SWORD

    C. ASKED HIS SERVANT TO DO IT

5. HOW DID GOD GUARD THE WAY TO THE TREE OF LIFE?

GENESIS 3:24

    A. PUT GATES AROUND IT

    B. MADE IT INVISIBLE

    C. SENT CHERUBIMS AND A FLAMING SWORD

6. HOW DID GOD CREATE THE FIRST WOMAN?

GENESIS 2:21-22

    A. OUT OF DUST

    B. OUT OF ADAM'S RIB

    C. OUT OF ADAM'S SHOULDER

FILL IN THE BLANKS

" ANYTHING I SAW AND
——————, I GOT FOR
——————. I DID NOT
—————— ———
PLEASURE I ————————
I WAS —————————— WITH
EVERYTHING I DID. AND THIS
PLEASURE WAS THE ————————
FOR ALL MY HARD ————. "

ECCLESIASTES 2:10

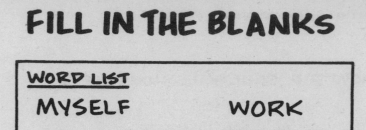

94

FILL IN THE BLANKS

WORD LIST

WHAT	GAIN
JUST	I
WIND	HARD
CHASING	TIME

" BUT THEN __ LOOKED AT _ _ _ _ _
I HAD DONE. I THOUGHT ABOUT
ALL THE _ _ _ _ WORK.
SUDDENLY I REALIZED IT WAS
_ _ _ _ A WASTE OF _ _ _ _ ,
LIKE _ _ _ _ _ _ _
THE _ _ _ _ ! THERE IS
NOTHING TO _ _ _ _ FROM
ANYTHING WE DO HERE ON
EARTH. "

ECCLESIASTES 2:11

FILL IN THE BLANKS

WORD LIST

FINAL	NOW
HONOR	OBEY
COMMANDS	MOST
PEOPLE	HEARD

" _ _ _ _ EVERYTHING HAS BEEN _ _ _ _ _ _ _ . HERE IS MY _ _ _ _ _ _ ADVICE: _ _ _ _ _ _ GOD AND _ _ _ _ _ HIS _ _ _ _ _ _ _ _ _ . THIS IS THE _ _ _ _ IMPORTANT THING _ _ _ _ _ _ _ CAN DO. "

ECCLESIASTES 12:13

FILL IN THE BLANKS

WORD LIST

EVERYTHING	PLAN
HIS	WORKS
LOVE	PEOPLE
GOD	KNOW

" WE _ _ _ _ THAT IN

_ _ _ _ _ _ _ _ _ _

GOD _ _ _ _ _ FOR THE

GOOD OF THOSE WHO _ _ _ _

HIM. THEY ARE THE

_ _ _ _ _ _ _ _ _

CALLED, BECAUSE THAT WAS

_ _ _ _ _ _ _ . "

ROMANS 8:28

97

MATCH THE SAYING

MATCH THE SAYING BELOW WITH THE
PERSON WHO SAID IT FROM THE
FOLLOWING PAGE.

1. "...I COME AGAINST YOU IN THE NAME OF
   THE LORD ALMIGHTY..."

   1 SAMUEL 17:45

   _____

2. " MANY WHO HAVE THE HIGHEST PLACE
   NOW WILL HAVE THE LOWEST PLACE
   IN THE FUTURE."

   MARK 10:29-31

   _____

3. " TO THOSE WHO ARE PURE, ALL
   THINGS ARE PURE."

   TITUS 1:1,15

   _____

4. " COME HERE. I'LL FEED YOUR BODY
   TO THE BIRDS OF THE AIR AND THE
   WILD ANIMALS."

   1 SAMUEL 17:23-44

   _____

5. " LOOK! I SEE HEAVEN OPEN. AND I SEE THE
   SON OF MAN STANDING AT GOD'S RIGHT SIDE."

   ACTS 7:56

   _____

JESUS   JEREMIAH

PAUL   SAUL

JOHN   GOD

GOLIATH   DAVID

JEROBOAM   STEPHEN

FILL IN THE BLANKS

WHY THE BOOK OF PROVERBS IS
IMPORTANT TO READ.

" THEY _____ WISDOM AND
SELF - _____ . THEY GIVE
UNDERSTANDING. THEY WILL
TEACH YOU HOW TO BE _____
AND SELF-CONTROLLED. THEY
WILL TEACH YOU WHAT IS
_____ AND FAIR AND
_____ . THEY GIVE THE
ABILITY TO _____ TO THOSE
WITH LITTLE KNOWLEDGE.
THEY GIVE KNOWLEDGE AND
GOOD _____ TO THE _____."

PROVERBS 1:2-4

WORD LIST

CONTROL	THINK
HONEST	TEACH
SENSE	RIGHT
WISE	YOUNG

TRUE / FALSE

1. SAMSON LED THE NATION OF ISRAEL FOR FIFTEEN YEARS.

   JUDGES 16:31   TRUE ____ FALSE ____

2. WHEN THE SOLDIERS SAW THE ANGEL AT THE TOMB OF JESUS, THEY BECAME LIKE DEAD MEN.

   MATTHEW 28:2-4   TRUE ____ FALSE ____

3. THIRD JOHN IS THE TWENTY-FIFTH BOOK IN THE NEW TESTAMENT.

                        TRUE ____ FALSE ____

CONT'D NEXT PAGE...

4. CORNELIUS' OCCUPATION WAS TENT-MAKING.

   ACTS 10:1   TRUE ____ FALSE ____

5. WE BECOME CHILDREN OF GOD BY PUTTING OUR FAITH IN JESUS CHRIST.

   GALATIANS 3:26   TRUE ____ FALSE ____

6. JOHN THE BAPTIST CALLED HIMSELF A VOICE.

   MARK 1:2-3   TRUE ____ FALSE ____

MATCH THE ANSWERS

MATCH THE ANSWERS ON THE FOLLOWING
PAGE TO THE QUESTIONS BELOW.

1. WHO ASKED, " WHAT CRIME HAS JESUS
   COMMITTED ? "

   _____   MARK 15: 14

2. WHO ASKED WHY JESUS ATE WITH THE
   TAX COLLECTORS AND SINNERS ?

                                MATTHEW 9:11

   _____

3. WHO SAID, " IT IS NOT THE HEALTHY WHO
   NEED A DOCTOR, BUT THE SICK " ?

                                MATTHEW 9:12

   _____

4. WHO SAID, "COME HERE, I'LL FEED YOUR
   BODY TO THE BIRDS OF THE AIR AND THE
   WILD ANIMALS " ?

                                1 SAMUEL 17: 4-44

   _____

5. WHO ASKED, "AM I MY BROTHER'S
   KEEPER ? "

                                GENESIS 4:9

   _____

6. WHO ASKED, " WHY HAVEN'T YOU TAKEN
   CARE OF GOD'S TEMPLE ? "

                                NEHEMIAH 1:1 ; 13:11

   _____

MARK	PHARISEES
ABEL	JAMES
HOSEA	CAIN
GOLIATH	PILATE
ISAAC	SAUL
NEHEMIAH	JESUS

MULTIPLE CHOICE

CIRCLE THE CORRECT ANSWER.

1. WHICH PROPHET MARRIED AN UNFAITHFUL WIFE NAMED GOMER?

    A. ISAIAH

    B. HOSEA

    C. JEREMIAH

    (ANSWER FOUND IN VERSE 2-3 OF ONE OF THE ABOVE CHOICES.)

2. WHO WAS ABRAHAM'S SECOND SON?

    GENESIS 21:2-3

    A. ISAAC

    B. ISHMAEL

    C. CAIN

3. THE MAGI WERE ...

    A. SOLDIERS.   MATTHEW 2:11-12

    B. WISE MEN OR KINGS.

    C. SHEPHERDS.

CONT'D NEXT PAGE ...

4. WHAT DOES THE LORD PREPARE IN THE PRESENCE OF OUR ENEMIES?

PSALM 23:5

    A. OUR CLOTHES

    B. DINNER

    C. A TABLE

5. IN THE PARABLE OF THE SOWER, WHERE DID THE SEED FALL THAT WAS CHOKED?

MATTHEW 13:7

    A. ON ROCKY SOIL

    B. AMONG THORNS

    C. AMONG WEEDS

6. WHERE DID LAZARUS, MARTHA, AND MARY LIVE?

JOHN 11:1

    A. JERUSALEM

    B. BETHANY

    C. NAZARETH

FILL IN THE BLANKS

WORD LIST

LOVED   KINGDOM

BELIEVES   CHILDREN

LIFE   LOVES

BORN   LIKE

1. "FOR GOD _____ THE WORLD SO MUCH THAT HE GAVE HIS ONLY SON. GOD GAVE HIS SON SO THAT WHOEVER _____ IN HIM MAY NOT BE LOST BUT HAVE ETERNAL _____."

JOHN 3:16

2. "I TELL YOU THE TRUTH. UNLESS ONE IS _____ AGAIN, HE CAN- NOT BE IN GOD'S _____."

JOHN 3:3

3. "YOU ARE GOD'S _____ WHOM HE _____. SO TRY TO BE _____ GOD."

EPHESIANS 5:1

107

FILL IN THE BLANKS

1. "MY BROTHERS, YOU WILL HAVE MANY
   _____ . BUT WHEN THESE THINGS
   _____ , YOU SHOULD BE VERY
   _____ . "

   JAMES 1:2

2. "I TOLD YOU THESE THINGS SO THAT
   YOU CAN HAVE PEACE IN ME. IN THIS
   _____ YOU WILL HAVE TROUBLE.
   BUT BE BRAVE! I HAVE _____
   THE WORLD! "

   JOHN 16:33

3. " IF ANY OF YOU NEEDS _____ , YOU
   SHOULD ASK GOD FOR IT. GOD IS
   _____ . HE ENJOYS GIVING TO ALL
   PEOPLE, SO HE WILL _____ YOU WISDOM."

   JAMES 1:5

MULTIPLE CHOICE
CIRCLE THE CORRECT ANSWER

1. THE SHORTEST CHAPTER IN THE BIBLE IS...

    A. PHILEMON 1.

    B. PSALM 117.

    C. TITUS 3.

2. WHO WAS CHOSEN TO REPLACE JUDAS ISCARIOT AFTER HE HANGED HIMSELF?

    ACTS 1: 23-26

    A. JAMES

    B. MATTHIAS

    C. ANDREW

3. WHO WAS A " WILD DONKEY OF A MAN "?

    GENESIS 16:11-12

    A. ISAAC

    B. JOHN

    C. ISHMAEL

CONT'D NEXT PAGE ...

4. WHAT EVANGELIST HAD FOUR DAUGHTERS WHO PROPHESIED?

ACTS 21:8-9

    A. ABRAHAM

    B. PHILIP

    C. ZACCHAEUS

5. AT WHAT HOUR OF THE DAY DID JESUS DIE?

MARK 15:34-3

    A. THE THIRD HOUR

    B. THE NINTH HOUR

    C. THE SIXTH HOUR

6. HOW TALL WAS GOLIATH?

1 SAMUEL 17:4

    A. OVER EIGHT FEET

    B. OVER NINE FEET

    C. OVER TEN FEET

FILL IN THE BLANKS

EPHESIANS 6:13-17 IS ABOUT THE ARMOR OF GOD.

1. THE BELT OF _____ .

2. THE BREASTPLATE OF

   _____ .

3. FEET FITTED WITH _____ .

4. THE SHIELD OF _____ .

5. THE HELMET OF _____ .

6. THE SWORD OF THE _____ .

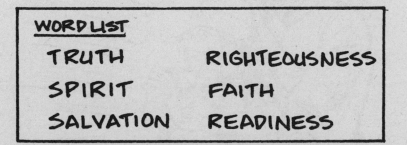

WORD LIST

TRUTH	RIGHTEOUSNESS
SPIRIT	FAITH
SALVATION	READINESS

WHO WAS HIS MOTHER?

MATCH SON TO MOTHER BY
DRAWING A LINE FROM ONE
NAME TO ANOTHER.

SOLOMON   RUTH
                                    RUTH 4:13-17

SAMUEL   HAGAR
                                    GENESIS 16:15

OBED   BATHSHEBA
                                    2 SAMUEL 12:24

ISHMAEL   ADAH
                                    GENESIS 36:4

ELIPHAZ   HANNAH
                                    1 SAMUEL 1:20

TRUE / FALSE

1. MATTHIAS REPLACED PETER AS AN APOSTLE.

    ACTS 1: 24-26

    TRUE _____ FALSE _____

2. PHILIP BAPTIZED AN ETHIOPIAN EUNUCH.

    ACTS 8:38

    TRUE _____ FALSE _____

3. THE DEATH OF THE FIRST BORN WAS ONE OF THE PLAGUES OF EGYPT.

    EXODUS 11: 4-6

    TRUE _____ FALSE _____

4. JESUS SAID A PROPHET HAS HONOR IN HIS OWN TOWN.

    MATTHEW 13:55-58

    TRUE _____ FALSE _____

CONT'D NEXT PAGE...

5. WHEN ABRAHAM DIED, GOD BLESSED HIS SON, ISAAC.

GENESIS 25:11

TRUE _____ FALSE _____

6. ABRAHAM WAS TESTED BY GOD.

GENESIS 22:1

TRUE _____ FALSE _____

7. THE QUEEN OF SHEBA CAME TO VISIT SOLOMON SO SHE COULD MARRY HIM.

1 KINGS 10:1-2

TRUE _____ FALSE _____

THE TEN COMMANDMENTS

NUMBER THEM SO THEY ARE IN THE RIGHT ORDER.

EXODUS 20: 3-17

_____ YOU SHALL NOT MAKE FOR YOURSELVES ANY IDOLS.

_____ YOU SHALL NOT LIE AGAINST YOUR NEIGHBOR.

_____ YOU MUST NOT MURDER ANYONE.

_____ YOU SHALL NOT STEAL.

_____ YOU MUST NOT BE GUILTY OF ADULTERY.

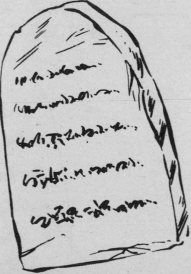

CONT'D NEXT PAGE...

_____ YOU SHALL NOT COVET ANYTHING BELONGING TO YOUR NEIGHBOR.

_____ YOU SHALL HAVE NO OTHER GODS BEFORE ME.

_____ YOU MUST NOT USE THE NAME OF THE LORD YOUR GOD THOUGHTLESSLY.

_____ REMEMBER THE SABBATH BY KEEPING IT HOLY.

_____ HONOR YOUR FATHER AND MOTHER.

FILL IN THE BLANKS

WORD LIST

LOVE	SOUL
NEIGHBOR	HEART
LORD	MIND
GOD	YOURSELF

"_____ THE _____ YOUR _____ WITH ALL YOUR _____ AND WITH ALL YOUR _____ AND WITH ALL YOUR _____."

MATTHEW 22:37

" LOVE YOUR _____ AS YOU LOVE _____."

MATTHEW 22:39

FILL IN THE BLANKS

WORD LIST

ADVICE   CHAIN
TEACHING   FATHER'S
LISTEN   MOTHER'S
FLOWERS   LIFE

" MY CHILD, _____ TO YOUR
_____ _____, AND
DO NOT FORGET YOUR _____
_____ ."

" THEIR TEACHING WILL BEAUTIFY
YOUR _____. IT WILL BE LIKE
_____ IN YOUR HAIR OR
A _____ AROUND YOUR
NECK."

PROVERBS 1: 8,9

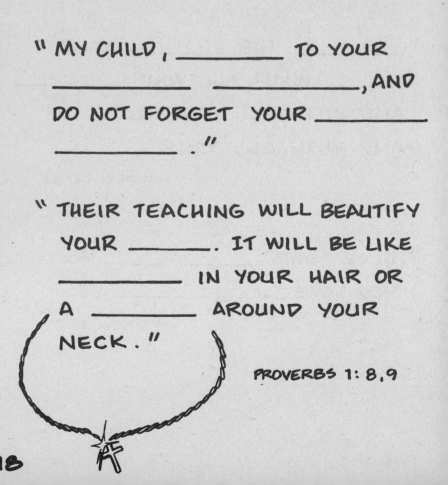

MATCH THE ANSWERS

MATCH THE ANSWERS ON THE FOLLOWING
PAGE TO THE QUESTIONS BELOW.

1. WHERE WAS RUTH'S HOMELAND?

   RUTH 1:1-7

   _____

2. WHO WAS THE THIRD SON OF ADAM?

   GENESIS 5:3

   _____

3. WHERE WAS JACOB BURIED?

   GENESIS 50:12-14

   _____

4. WHO SAID, "IF ANYONE IS NOT WITH
   ME, THEN HE IS AGAINST ME"?

   MATTHEW 12:30

   _____

5. WHO WAS HOSEA'S FATHER?

   HOSEA 1:1

   _____

6. IN THE GOSPEL OF JOHN, WHO DID
   JESUS WEEP FOR?

   JOHN 11:31-35

   _____

ISAIAH   ESAU
SETH   MOAB
JESUS   CANAAN
JUDAH   PAUL
MARTHA   BEERI
LAZARUS   MARY

MATCH THE ANSWERS

MATCH THE ANSWERS ON THE FOLLOWING
PAGE TO THE QUESTIONS BELOW.

1. WHO WAS THE FIRST CHRISTIAN
   MARTYR?

   _____ ACTS 7:59-60

2. WHAT TWELVE-YEAR-OLD GIRL WAS
   BROUGHT BACK TO LIFE BY JESUS?

   _____ LUKE 8:40-56

3. WHO GAVE MOSES HIS NAME?

   _____ EXODUS 2:10

4. WHO TOLD NOAH TO COME OUT OF
   THE ARK?

   _____ GENESIS 8:15-16

5. IN WHAT TOWN WAS JETHRO A
   PRIEST?

   _____ EXODUS 18:1

6. WHAT WAS THE NAME OF THE
   CENTURION PAUL WAS HANDED OVER
   TO?

   _____ ACTS 27:1

PAUL

JAIRUS' DAUGHTER

HIS MOTHER

PHARAOH'S DAUGHTER

GOD

CORNELIUS

PETER'S DAUGHTER

JULIUS

HIS WIFE

MIDIAN

JERUSALEM

STEPHEN

MULTIPLE CHOICE

CIRCLE THE CORRECT ANSWER.

1. WHAT HAPPENED WHEN PHARAOH WOULD NOT LET MOSES AND HIS PEOPLE GO?

   EXODUS 13:15

   A. EVERY FIRSTBORN DIED.

   B. EVERY SECONDBORN DIED.

   C. THE RIVER DRIED UP.

2. TO WHAT DID PAUL COMPARE THE COMING OF "THE DAY OF THE LORD"?

   1 THESSALONIANS 5:2

   A. A ROAR OF THUNDER

   B. A FLASH OF LIGHTNING

   C. A THIEF IN THE NIGHT

3. WHAT HAPPENED TO PETER WHEN JESUS ASKED HIM TO WALK ON WATER?

   MATTHEW 14: 29-31

   A. HE DROWNED.

   B. HE SANK FOR LACK OF FAITH.

   C. AN ANGEL CARRIED HIM.

CONT'D NEXT PAGE ...

4. WHO WAS BLINDED BY JESUS ON THE WAY TO DAMASCUS?

ACTS 9:8

    A. PAUL

    B. SAUL

    C. PETER

5. WHO DID THE LORD CALL BY A VISION IN DAMASCUS?

ACTS 9:10

    A. ANANIAS

    B. PETER

    C. PAUL

6. WHAT DID THE ANGEL MEASURE THE CITY WITH?

REVELATION 21:16

    A. A MEASURING TAPE

    B. A STICK

    C. A SQUARE AS LONG AS WIDE AND HIGH

FILL IN THE BLANKS

" MY _____ , BELIEVE WHAT
I _____ AND _____
WHAT I _____ YOU.
_____ TO _____. TRY
WITH ALL YOUR _____ TO
GAIN _____ ."

PROVERBS 2:1-2

FILL IN THE BLANKS

" ONLY THE _____ GIVES _____ . _____ AND UNDERSTANDING COME FROM _____ . HE STORES UP WISDOM FOR THOSE WHO ARE _____ . LIKE A _____ HE _____ THOSE WHO ARE _____ . "

PROVERBS 2:6-7

MULTIPLE CHOICE

CIRCLE THE CORRECT ANSWER.

1. WHAT WAS THE FIRST TREE MENTIONED IN THE BIBLE?

   GENESIS 2:9

   A. APPLE

   B. CEDAR

   C. TREE OF LIFE

2. HOW OLD WAS JOSHUA WHEN HE DIED?

   JOSHUA 24:29

   A. ONE HUNDRED AND TEN

   B. ONE HUNDRED AND TWELVE

   C. SIXTY-SEVEN

3. WHO WAS MARY'S FATHER-IN-LAW?

   MATTHEW 1:16

   A. DAVID

   B. ZECHARIAH

   C. JACOB

CONT'D NEXT PAGE...

4. WHOSE BONES WERE CARRIED FORTY YEARS THROUGH THE DESERT?

JOSHUA 24:32

    A. MOSES'

    B. JOSEPH'S

    C. ADAM'S

5. WHAT DID JAMES SAY MAN COULD NOT TAME?

JAMES 3:8

    A. A BEAR

    B. A LION

    C. THE TONGUE

6. HOW LONG WAS JONAH IN THE BELLY OF THE FISH?

MATTHEW 12:40

    A. THREE DAYS AND NIGHTS

    B. SEVEN DAYS AND NIGHTS

    C. THIRTY DAYS AND NIGHTS

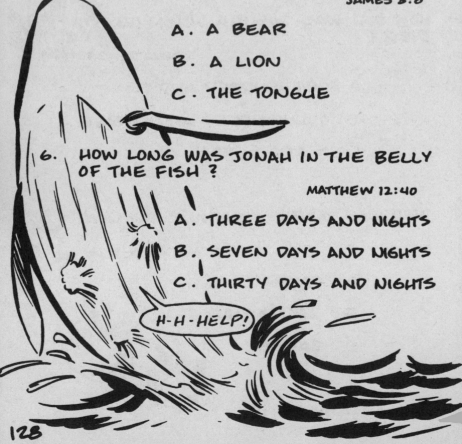

MULTIPLE CHOICE

CIRCLE THE CORRECT ANSWER.

1. WHY DID MOSES BREAK THE TABLETS OF THE TEN COMMANDMENTS?

   EXODUS 32:19

   A. THEY WERE TOO HEAVY.

   B. HE DROPPED THEM.

   C. HE WAS ANGRY AT THE ISRAELITES.

2. WHAT WAS THE SIGN OF THE PROMISE BETWEEN GOD AND NOAH?

   GENESIS 9:12-13

   A. A RAINBOW

   B. THE RAIN

   C. THE ARK

3. WHAT DOES THE NAME "EVE" MEAN?

   GENESIS 3:20

   A. MOTHER OF EVENING

   B. MOTHER OF ALL LIVING

   C. BEGINNING OF NIGHT

CONT'D NEXT PAGE...

4. WHAT IS THE FOURTEENTH BOOK OF THE OLD TESTAMENT ?

    A. SECOND CHRONICLES

    B. FIRST CHRONICLES

    C. SECOND KINGS

5. WHAT HAPPENED TO THE YOUTH THAT MADE FUN OF ELISHA'S BALDNESS ?

    2 KINGS 2:23-24

    A. THEY WERE SENT TO THEIR ROOMS.

    B. THEY WERE MAULED BY BEARS.

    C. THEY HAD TO APOLOGIZE.

6. HOW OLD WAS JEHORAM WHEN HE BECAME KING OF JUDAH ?

    2 CHRONICLES 21:5

    A. TWELVE

    B. THIRTY-TWO

    C. TWENTY-FIVE

UNSCRAMBLE THE VERSE

TO FIND OUT WHAT THE VERSE BELOW SAYS, FILL IN THE BLANKS. ALL THE VOWELS ARE THERE. ALL YOU NEED TO DO IS ADD THE CONSONANTS.

" YM DCHLI , OD TNO TFEORG YM

GTNEIAHC. NTHE UOY IWLL

ELVI A GNLO MTEI. DNA RYUO

EIFL LILW EB SLSUUFCSCE. "

" __ __I__, _O _O_

_O__E_ __

_EA__I__.

__E_ __OU_I__

_I_ E A _O__

_I_E. A___

_OU_ _I_E_I__

_E _U__E___U_."

PROVERBS 3:1-2

UNSCRAMBLE THE VERSE

TO FIND OUT WHAT THE VERSE BELOW SAYS, FILL IN THE BLANKS. ALL THE VOWELS ARE THERE. ALL YOU NEED TO DO IS ADD THE CONSONANTS.

"TTSUR HET DLRO TWHI LAL RUYO THARE. DTON DNDEPE NO RYUO NOW DRENUNSINDTAG. RREMMEBE ETH DLOR NI EEVYRGNIHT UYO OD. DNA EH LLWI EIGV YUO SSSCCEU."

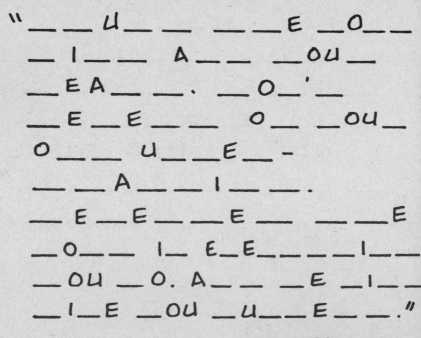

"__ U__ __ __ __E __O__ __
_ I__ __ A__ __ __OU__
__E A__ __. __O__'__
__E __E __ __ O__ __OU__
O__ __ U__ __E__-
__ __A__ __ I__ __.
__ E __E __ __ E __ __ __E
__O__ __ I__ E__E__ __ __ __I__ __
__OU __O. A__ __ __E __I__
__I__E __OU __U__ __E__ __."

TRUE / FALSE

1. MARY, JESUS' MOTHER, WAS NOT
   AT THE CRUCIFIXION.

   JOHN 19:25

   TRUE ____ FALSE ____

2. JESUS HAD NO BROTHERS OR
   SISTERS.

   MARK 6:3

   TRUE ____ FALSE ____

3. ISAIAH WAS AN APOSTLE.

   2 CHRONICLES 32:20

   TRUE ____ FALSE ____

CONT'D NEXT PAGE...

4. JESUS WAS TWELVE YEARS OLD WHEN HE FIRST SPOKE AT THE TEMPLE.

    LUKE 2: 42-46

    TRUE ____ FALSE ____

5. BARNABAS WAS A FOLLOWER OF JESUS.

    ACTS 11: 22-24

    TRUE ____ FALSE ____

6. KING DAVID MOVED THE ARK OF THE COVENANT FROM THE HOUSE OF ABINADAB TO THE TABERNACLE.

    2 SAMUEL 6: 2-17

    TRUE ____ FALSE ____

TRUE / FALSE

1. SOLOMON WAS DAVID'S SON.

   1 KINGS 2:1

   TRUE _____ FALSE _____

2. DAVID KILLED SIX HUNDRED OF THE ARAMEAN CHARIOTEERS AND THIRTY THOUSAND OF THEIR FOOT SOLDIERS.

   2 SAMUEL 10:18

   TRUE _____ FALSE _____

3. ABRAHAM WAS TESTED BY GOD.

   GENESIS 22:1

   TRUE _____ FALSE _____

CONT'D NEXT PAGE ...

4. GOD DESTROYED SODOM AND
GOMORRAH.

GENESIS 19:24

TRUE ____ FALSE ____

5. SIMON THE SORCERER BECAME A
FOLLOWER OF JESUS CHRIST.

ACTS 8:13

TRUE ____ FALSE ____

6. ELISABETH, WIFE OF ZACHARIAS,
WAS A DESCENDANT OF AARON.

LUKE 1:5

TRUE ____ FALSE ____

MATCH THE ANSWERS

MATCH THE ANSWERS ON THE FOLLOWING
PAGE TO THE QUESTIONS BELOW.

1. WHAT DID EZEKIEL EAT THAT WAS AS
   SWEET AS HONEY ?

   EZEKIEL 3:3

   _____

2. WHO WAS TOLD IN A VISION ABOUT
   HIS SON'S BIRTH ?

   LUKE 1: 11-13

   _____

3. IN WHAT PROVINCE DID JESUS MEET
   THE FISHERMEN ?

   MATTHEW 4: 18-19

   _____

4. WHERE WAS JACOB BURIED ?

   GENESIS 50: 12-14

   _____

5. WHO WAS SOLOMON'S MOTHER ?

   1 KINGS 1:11

   _____

6. WHAT IS THE LAST WORD IN THE
   BIBLE ?

   REVELATION 22: 21

   _____

ZACHARIAS	A HONEYCOMB
QUEEN OF SHEBA	JOSEPH
THE SCROLL	GALILEE
JERUSALEM	BATHSHEBA
JUDAH	EGYPT
THE END	AMEN

MATCH THE ANSWERS

MATCH THE ANSWERS ON THE FOLLOWING
PAGE TO THE QUESTIONS BELOW.

1. WHERE WAS JESUS BORN?

   LUKE 2:4-6

   _____

2. WHAT BABY WAS FOUND IN A BASKET
   IN A RIVER?

   EXODUS 2:3-10

   _____

3. WHAT WAS THE THIRD PLAGUE THE
   LORD BROUGHT ON PHARAOH?

   EXODUS 8:16-19

   _____

4. WHO WAS AARON'S SISTER?

   EXODUS 15:20

   _____

5. IN WHAT CITY WAS RAHAB AND THOSE
   IN HER HOUSE THE ONLY SURVIVORS?

   JOSHUA 6:17-25

   _____

6. IN WHAT MONTH DID THE ARK COME
   TO REST ON MOUNT ARARAT?

   GENESIS 8:4

   _____

EGYPT   NAZARETH
AARON   MOSES
BETHLEHEM   PLAGUE OF LICE
PLAGUE OF FROGS ZIPPORAH
SEVENTH MONTH MIRIAM
JERICHO   EIGHTH MONTH

MULTIPLE CHOICE

CIRCLE THE CORRECT ANSWER.

1. HOW MANY CHARIOTS AND HORSEMEN DID SOLOMON HAVE?

   1 KINGS 10:26

   A. FOURTEEN HUNDRED CHARIOTS TWELVE THOUSAND HORSEMEN

   B. TWELVE THOUSAND CHARIOTS FOURTEEN THOUSAND HORSEMEN

   C. TWELVE THOUSAND CHARIOTS FOURTEEN HUNDRED HORSEMEN

2. WHERE DID ADAM AND EVE FIRST LIVE?

   GENESIS 2:8

   A. BABYLON

   B. GARDEN OF EDEN

   C. ISRAEL

3. WHAT DID PAUL HAVE IN TROAS?

   ACTS 16:8-9

   A. A COLD

   B. A DREAM

   C. A VISION

CONT'D NEXT PAGE ...

4. THE NAME "ABRAHAM" MEANS...?

GENESIS 17:5

    A. FATHER OF NATIONS

    B. FATHER OF ISAAC

    C. FATHER OF ALL

5. HOW MANY DAYS DID WATER FLOOD THE EARTH?

GENESIS 7:24

    A. SEVEN DAYS

    B. THIRTY DAYS

    C. ONE HUNDRED AND FIFTY DAYS

6. HOW MANY PEOPLE WERE KILLED WHEN SAMSON DESTROYED THE TEMPLE OF DAGON?

JUDGES 16:22-30

    A. THREE THOUSAND

    B. THIRTY THOUSAND

    C. THREE HUNDRED THOUSAND

MULTIPLE CHOICE
CIRCLE THE CORRECT ANSWER.

1. WHAT HAPPENED TO PHARAOH'S ARMY WHEN THEY CHASED AFTER MOSES AND HIS PEOPLE?

    EXODUS 14:26-28

    A. THEY GOT SAND IN THEIR EYES.

    B. THEY GOT TIRED OF THE CHASE.

    C. THEY DROWNED IN THE RED SEA.

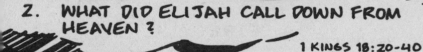

2. WHAT DID ELIJAH CALL DOWN FROM HEAVEN?

    1 KINGS 18:20-40

    A. FIRE

    B. RAIN

    C. ANGELS

3. HOW DID JUDAS IDENTIFY JESUS FOR THE SOLDIERS?

    MATTHEW 26:48-49

    A. BY POINTING HIM OUT

    B. WITH A KISS

    C. BY A HAND ON HIS SHOULDER

CONT'D NEXT PAGE ...

143

4. **WHAT LESSON DID JESUS TEACH THE DISCIPLES BY WASHING THEIR FEET?**

JOHN 13:5-16

    A. TO KEEP THEIR FEET CLEAN

    B. TO SERVE OTHERS HUMBLY

    C. ABOUT CEREMONIAL CLEANSING

5. **WHAT DID GOD CREATE TO SEPARATE DAY FROM NIGHT?**

GENESIS 1:14-19

    A. FIRE

    B. LIGHTS (STARS) IN THE SKY

    C. ELECTRIC LIGHTS

6. **FINISH PAUL'S SENTENCE, "ALL PEOPLE HAVE SINNED AND..."**

ROMANS 3:23

    A. ARE NOT GOOD ENOUGH FOR GOD'S GLORY.

    B. SHOULD BE PUNISHED.

    C. NEED FORGIVENESS.

FINISH THE VERSE

TO FIND OUT WHAT THE VERSE BELOW SAYS, FILL IN THE BLANKS. ALL THE CONSONANTS ARE THERE. ALL YOU NEED TO DO IS ADD THE VOWELS.

VOWELS : A E I O U

"D__N'T D_P_ND __N
Y__ _R __WN W_SD_M,
R__SP__CT TH_ L_RD
__ND R_F_S__T_ D_
WR__NG. TH__N Y__ _R
B_DY W__LL B_
H___LTHY __ND Y__ _R
B__N__S W__LL B_
STR__NG."

PROVERBS 3:7-8

145

FINISH THE VERSE

TO FIND OUT WHAT THE VERSE BELOW SAYS, FILL IN THE BLANKS. ALL THE CONSONANTS ARE THERE. ALL YOU NEED TO DO IS ADD THE VOWELS.

VOWELS: A E I O U

" MY CH_LD, D_ N_T R_J_CT TH_ L_RD'S D_SC_PL_N_. _ND D_N'T B_ _NGRY WH_N H_ C_RR_CTS Y___. TH_ L_RD C_RR_CTS TH_S_ H_ L_V_S, J_ST _S _ F_TH_R C_RR_CTS TH_ CH_LD TH_T H_ L_V_S. "

PROVERBS 3:11-12

TRUE / FALSE

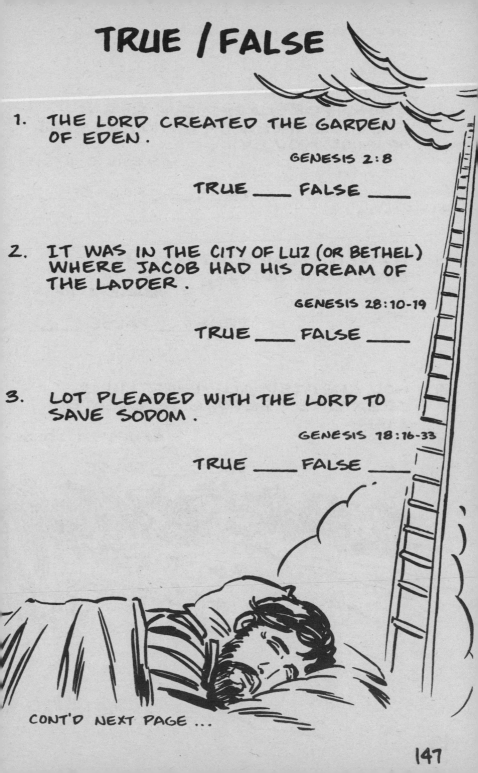

1. THE LORD CREATED THE GARDEN
   OF EDEN.

   GENESIS 2:8

   TRUE ____ FALSE ____

2. IT WAS IN THE CITY OF LUZ (OR BETHEL)
   WHERE JACOB HAD HIS DREAM OF
   THE LADDER.

   GENESIS 28:10-19

   TRUE ____ FALSE ____

3. LOT PLEADED WITH THE LORD TO
   SAVE SODOM.

   GENESIS 18:16-33

   TRUE ____ FALSE ____

CONT'D NEXT PAGE ...

4. ADAM PERSUADED EVE TO EAT FROM THE TREE OF THE KNOWLEDGE OF GOOD AND EVIL.

GENESIS 3:6

TRUE ____ FALSE ____

5. A RIVER FLOWED OUT OF THE GARDEN OF EDEN.

GENESIS 2:10

TRUE ____ FALSE ____

6. GOD CREATED ALL OTHER LIVING CREATURES BEFORE HE CREATED MAN.

GENESIS 1:20-26

TRUE ____ FALSE ____

TRUE / FALSE

1. TROPHIMUS WAS THOUGHT TO HAVE BEEN
   BROUGHT INTO THE TEMPLE WITH PAUL.
   ACTS 21:26-29

   TRUE _____ FALSE _____

2. TROPHIMUS WAS AN EGYPTIAN.
   ACTS 21:29

   TRUE _____ FALSE _____

3. JETHRO WAS MOSES' SON-IN-LAW.
   EXODUS 18:12

   TRUE _____ FALSE _____

CONT'D NEXT PAGE ...

4. AFTER JESUS HAD FASTED IN THE WILDERNESS, ANGELS MINISTERED TO HIM.

MATTHEW 4:11

TRUE _____ FALSE _____

5. THE LAKE OF FIRE IS THE SECOND DEATH IN THE BOOK OF REVELATION.

REVELATION 20:14

TRUE _____ FALSE _____

6. PAUL DID NOT VISIT ICONIUM TO PREACH THE GOSPEL.

ACTS 13:50-14:1

TRUE _____ FALSE _____

MATCH THE ANSWERS

MATCH THE ANSWERS ON THE FOLLOWING
PAGE TO THE QUESTIONS BELOW.

1. WHO ROLLED BACK THE STONE FROM
   JESUS' TOMB?

   MATTHEW 28:2

   _____

2. IN WHAT CITY THAT PAUL VISITED WAS
   THERE A SIGN THAT READ, "TO A GOD
   WHO IS NOT KNOWN"?

   ACTS 17: 22-23

   _____

3. WHO HAD A VISION OF A GREAT THRONE
   SURROUNDED BY TWENTY-FOUR
   ELDERS?

   REVELATION 1:1; 4:4

   _____

4. WHAT WAS URIAH'S OCCUPATION?

   2 SAMUEL 11:15-17

   _____

5. WHO WAS THE MOTHER OF KING JOASH?

   2 CHRONICLES 24:1

   _____

6. HOW MANY WIVES DID KING JOASH HAVE?

   2 CHRONICLES 24:3

   _____

TWO   TWO HUNDRED

THE DISCIPLES   ATHENS

THESSALONICA   SOLDIER

PAUL   JOHN

TENTMAKER   ZIBIAH

JEHOSHEBA   THE ANGEL OF
              THE LORD

MATCH THE ANSWERS

MATCH THE ANSWERS ON THE FOLLOWING PAGE TO THE QUESTIONS BELOW.

1. WHO SAID, "LOOK! I SEE HEAVEN OPEN AND I SEE THE SON OF MAN STANDING AT GOD'S RIGHT SIDE" ?

ACTS 7:56-59

_____

2. WHO SANG, "GOD FILLS THE HUNGRY WITH GOOD THINGS, BUT HE SENDS THE RICH AWAY WITH NOTHING" ?

LUKE 1:46-53

_____

3. WHO CALLED HIS FOLLOWERS "THE SALT OF THE EARTH" ?

MATTHEW 4:23; 5:13

_____

4. IN WHAT LAND WAS PAUL FORBIDDEN TO PREACH BY THE HOLY SPIRIT ?

ACTS 16:6

_____

5. WHAT KIND OF SNAKE BIT THE APOSTLE PAUL ?

ACTS 28:3

_____

6. HOW OLD WAS ISAAC WHEN JACOB AND ESAU WERE BORN ?

GENESIS 25:26

_____

PAUL	MARY
ELISABETH	JOHN
JESUS	STEPHEN
VIPER	ASIA
GARDENER	POISONOUS
TWENTY-SIX	SIXTY

OUCH...

MULTIPLE CHOICE
CIRCLE THE CORRECT ANSWER

1. DANIEL WAS A ... ?

   MATTHEW 24:15

   A. PROPHET.

   B. DISCIPLE.

   C. APOSTLE.

2. WHO WAS MELCHIZEDEK ?

   GENESIS 14:18
   HEBREWS 5:10

   A. A PROPHET

   B. A PHARISEE

   C. A HIGH PRIEST

3. WHO IS BEELZEBUB ?

   MATTHEW 12:24-27

   A. SATAN

   B. A PROPHET

   C. A KING

CONT'D NEXT PAGE ...

4. HOW MANY BOOKS ARE IN THE NEW TESTAMENT?

    A. TWENTY

    B. TWENTY-SEVEN

    C. TWENTY-EIGHT

5. WHO WAS HOSEA'S FIRST SON?

HOSEA 1:3-4

    A. JEZREEL

    B. SIMON

    C. HOSEA, JR.

6. WHAT DID MOSES DO TO GET WATER OUT OF THE ROCK?

EXODUS 17:5-6

    A. HIT IT WITH A HAMMER

    B. STRUCK IT WITH HIS STAFF

    C. KICKED IT

MULTIPLE CHOICE
CIRCLE THE CORRECT ANSWER.

1. WHEN THE ISRAELITES SPOKE OUT AGAINST GOD AND MOSES IN THE DESERT, WHAT DID GOD SEND THEM?

   NUMBERS 21: 4-6

   A. POISONOUS SNAKES

   B. QUAIL

   C. MANNA

2. WHAT BROTHERS WERE GIVEN THE NAME, "SONS OF THUNDER"?

   MARK 3:17

   A. JOHN AND JAMES

   B. CAIN AND ABEL

   C. PEREZ AND ZERAH

3. JESUS TAUGHT IN PARABLES; WHAT IS A PARABLE?

   A. A BOOK OF MANY STORIES

   B. A RIDDLE

   C. A WAY OF TEACHING BY COMPARING THINGS TO GET THE MEANING

CONT'D NEXT PAGE ...

4. THE NAME "ISAAC" MEANS... ?

GENESIS 17:17
18:9-15

    A. ONE WHO LAUGHS.

    B. STRONG AND MIGHTY.

    C. GRATITUDE.

5. WHAT DOES THE NAME "ESAU" MEAN ?

GENESIS 25:25

    A. BALD

    B. HAIRY

    C. SLIM

6. WHAT TEMPLE DID SAMSON TEAR DOWN WHEN HE REGAINED HIS STRENGTH ?

JUDGES 16:22-30

    A. TEMPLE OF DAGON

    B. SYNAGOGUE

    C. JERUBBABEL'S TEMPLE

MATCH THE PARABLE

MATCH THE SCRIPTURE REFERENCE ON THE FOLLOWING PAGE TO THE PARABLE BELOW.

1. THE WISE AND FOOLISH BUILDERS.

   _____

2. THE MUSTARD SEED.

   _____

3. THE PEARL OF GREAT PRICE.

   _____

4. THE LOST SHEEP.

   _____

5. THE PRODIGAL SON.

   _____

6. THE WEDDING BANQUET.

   _____

7. THE GOOD SAMARITAN.

   _____

8. THE UNMERCIFUL SERVANT.

   _____

LUKE 15: 3-7

LUKE 7: 41-43

MATTHEW 7: 24-27

MATTHEW 22: 1-14

MATTHEW 18: 23-35

LUKE 15: 11-32

MARK 4: 30-32

LUKE 10: 30-37

LUKE 11: 5-8

LUKE 14: 7-11

MATTHEW 13: 45-46

LUKE 19: 11-27

FILL IN THE BLANKS

WORD LIST

WISDOM	SIGHT
OUT	REASON
LIFE	CHILD
NECKLACE	YOUR

" MY _____ , HOLD ON TO
_____ AND _____ .
DON'T LET THEM ___ OF
YOUR _____ . THEY WILL
GIVE YOU _____ . LIKE A
_____ THEY WILL
BEAUTIFY _____ LIFE. "

PROVERBS 3:21-22

FILL IN THE BLANKS

WORD LIST

PEACEFUL   DOWN

NEED   AFRAID

SLEEP   HURT

SAFETY   LIE

" THEN YOU WILL GO ON YOUR
WAY IN _____ . AND YOU
WILL NOT GET _____ . YOU
WON'T _____ TO BE
_____ WHEN YOU LIE
_____ . WHEN YOU ____
DOWN, YOUR _____ WILL
BE _____ .

PROVERBS 3: 23-24

ZZZZZ Z ZZ

FILL IN THE BLANKS

WORD LIST

KEEP	LORD
PEOPLE	GOOD
HELP	SAFE
TRAPPED	ABLE

" THE _____ WILL KEEP YOU _____ . HE WILL _____ YOU FROM BEING _____ . WHENEVER YOU ARE _____ , DO _____ TO _____ WHO NEED _____ . "

PROVERBS 3: 26-27

FILL IN THE BLANKS

WORD LIST

TEACH GOOD

UNDERSTAND TELLING

ATTENTION TEACHING

FORGET CHILDREN

" MY _____ , LISTEN TO YOUR

FATHER'S _____ . PAY

_____ SO YOU WILL

_____ . WHAT I AM

_____ YOU IS _____ .

DO NOT _____ WHAT I

_____ YOU. "

PROVERBS 4:1-2

MULTIPLE CHOICE

CIRCLE THE CORRECT ANSWER.

1. RIGHT AFTER JESUS WAS BAPTIZED A VOICE FROM HEAVEN SAID WHAT?
   MATTHEW 3:17

   A. "THIS IS MY SON AND I LOVE HIM. I AM VERY PLEASED WITH HIM."

   B. "THIS IS MY SON AND HE IS THE WAY TO HEAVEN."

   C. "THIS IS MY SON, FOLLOW HIM."

2. WHO ASKED JESUS WHETHER IT WAS RIGHT TO PAY TAXES TO THE ROMANS?
   MATTHEW 22: 15-21

   A. HIS PARENTS

   B. HIS DISCIPLES

   C. THE PHARISEES

3. HOW OLD WAS ENOCH WHEN THE LORD TOOK HIM?
   GENESIS 5: 23-24

   A. SIXTY-FIVE YEARS OLD

   B. THREE HUNDRED AND SIXTY-FIVE YEARS OLD

   C. SEVENTY YEARS OLD

CONT'D NEXT PAGE...

165

4. IN WHAT CITY WAS PAUL ALMOST WHIPPED FOR SPEAKING TO THE PEOPLE?

ACTS 22:22-29

    A. ROME

    B. JERUSALEM

    C. MACEDONIA

5. HOW MANY YEARS DID GOD ADD TO KING HEZEKIAH'S LIFE?

ISAIAH 38:5

    A. FIVE

    B. TEN

    C. FIFTEEN

6. HOW MANY YEARS DID THE ISRAELITES LIVE IN EGYPT?

EXODUS 12:40-41

    A. FOUR HUNDRED YEARS

    B. FOUR HUNDRED AND THIRTY YEARS

    C. FIVE HUNDRED YEARS

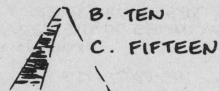

MULTIPLE CHOICE
CIRCLE THE CORRECT ANSWER.

1. WHERE DID MOSES GO AFTER KILLING THE EGYPTIAN?

   EXODUS 2:15

   A. HOME

   B. JUDAH

   C. MIDIAN

2. MOSES WAS WATCHING A FLOCK OF SHEEP WHEN THE LORD CAME TO HIM. WHOSE FLOCK WAS HE WATCHING?

   EXODUS 3:1

   A. THE KING'S

   B. HIS FATHER'S

   C. JETHRO'S

3. IN WHAT MONTH DID THE ANGEL APPEAR TO THE VIRGIN MARY?

   LUKE 1:26-27

   A. THIRD MONTH

   B. SIXTH MONTH

   C. NINTH MONTH

CONT'D NEXT PAGE...

4. WHO MADE HIS WIFE PASS AS HIS SISTER ?

GENESIS 20:2

    A. MOSES

    B. ABRAHAM

    C. ISAAC

5. WHAT WAS THE POTTER'S FIELD KNOWN AS ?

MATTHEW 27: 7-8

    A. FIELD OF BLOOD

    B. FIELD OF POTTERS

    C. FIELD OF DEATH

6. WHO TURNED HIS STAFF INTO A SNAKE ?

EXODUS 7:10

    A. MOSES

    B. AARON

    C. PAUL

MATCH THE ANSWERS

MATCH THE ANSWERS ON THE FOLLOWING
PAGE TO THE QUESTIONS BELOW.

1. WHO WAS EPHRAIM'S FATHER ?

   GENESIS 41:50-52

   _____

2. WHAT WAS HEZEKIAH'S
   OCCUPATION ?

   2 CHRONICLES 29:1

   _____

3. WHO WAS THE LAST PROPHET OF THE
   OLD TESTAMENT ?

   _____

4. ON WHAT MOUNTAIN DID MOSES
   RECEIVE THE TEN COMMANDMENTS ?

   EXODUS 19:20-20:17

   _____

5. WHERE DID NOAH'S ARK COME
   TO REST ?

   GENESIS 8:4

   _____

6. WHO PLAYED A MADMAN TO ESCAPE
   FROM HIS ENEMIES ?

   1 SAMUEL 21:12-15

   _____

KING	DAVID
MALACHI	JOSEPH
HAGGAI	AARON
MOUNTAINS OF ARARAT	PROPHET
PAUL	MOUNT SINAI
ISAAC	MOUNT OF OLIVES

MATCH THE ANSWERS

MATCH THE ANSWERS ON THE FOLLOWING
PAGE TO THE QUESTIONS BELOW.

1. HOW MANY JARS OF WATER DID
   JESUS CHANGE TO WINE?

   JOHN 2: 1-10

   _____

2. WHAT OBJECT BROUGHT JOSEPH'S
   BROTHERS BACK TO EGYPT?

   GENESIS 44: 1-13

   _____

3. HOW MANY BOOKS OF THE BIBLE DID
   JESUS WRITE?

   _____

4. AT WHAT AGE DID LAMECH DIE?

   GENESIS 5:31

   _____

   _____

5. WHO WAS LAMECH'S FATHER?

   GENESIS 5:25

   _____

6. WHAT PROPHET WAS COMMANDED BY
   GOD TO GO TO NINEVEH?

   JONAH 1: 1-2

   _____

SEVEN JARS

A SILVER CUP

FOUR

NONE

SIXTY-SEVEN

JONAH

JOB

SIX JARS

METHUSELAH

A SILVER SPOON

AMOS

SEVEN HUNDRED
AND SEVENTY-SEVE

TRUE / FALSE

1. AT THE PASSOVER FEAST, JESUS SAID THAT ONE PERSON WOULD BETRAY HIM.

    MATTHEW 26:21

    TRUE ____ FALSE ____

2. JESUS RODE ON A HORSE TO JERUSALEM.

    MATTHEW 21:7

    TRUE ____ FALSE ____

3. JOHN WROTE THE BOOK OF REVELATION WHILE IN ROME.

    REVELATION 1:1-9

    TRUE ____ FALSE ____

CONT'D NEXT PAGE ...

4. BARSABAS WAS AN APOSTLE.

ACTS 1: 23-26

TRUE _____ FALSE _____

5. ABRAHAM LEFT EVERYTHING TO HIS SON ISAAC WHEN HE DIED.

GENESIS 25:5

TRUE _____ FALSE _____

6. BECAUSE ESAU WANTED TO KILL JACOB, JACOB FLED TO HARAN.

GENESIS 27: 41-43

TRUE _____ FALSE _____

TRUE / FALSE

1. IT TOOK ELISHA JUST ONE TRY TO SET FIRE TO HIS WATER-DRENCHED SACRIFICE.

   1 KINGS 18:36-38

   TRUE _____ FALSE _____

2. SOLOMON WAS MADE KING BEFORE DAVID DIED.

   1 KINGS 1:43-48

   TRUE _____ FALSE _____

3. AARON DIED ON MOUNT HOR AFTER MOSES GAVE HIS PRIESTLY CLOTHES TO HIS SON.

   NUMBERS 20:27-28

   TRUE _____ FALSE _____

CONT'D NEXT PAGE . . .

4. **KING DARIUS HAD DANIEL TOSSED INTO THE LIONS' DEN.**

DANIEL 6:6-16

TRUE _____ FALSE _____

5. **NOAH'S SON JAPHETH WAS OLDER THAN HIS BROTHER SHEM.**

GENESIS 10:21

TRUE _____ FALSE _____

6. **JESUS WAS THIRTY-THREE YEARS OLD WHEN HE BEGAN HIS MINISTRY.**

LUKE 3:23

TRUE _____ FALSE _____

WHO SAID?

MATCH THE NAMES ON THE FOLLOWING
PAGE TO THE SAYINGS BELOW.

1. " BUT IF A MAN IS ALREADY OLD, HOW
   CAN HE BE BORN AGAIN ? "

   JOHN 3: 4

   _____

2. " I AM NOT GUILTY OF THIS MAN'S
   DEATH. YOU ARE THE ONES CAUSING
   IT. "

   MATTHEW 27:24

   _____

3. " YOU WILL NOT DIE. "

   GENESIS 3:4

   _____

4. " TEACHER , I WANT TO SEE."

   MARK 10:46-57

   _____

5. " HE MUST BECOME GREATER AND I
   MUST BECOME LESS IMPORTANT. "

   JOHN 3:23-30

   _____

6. " NO! YOU WILL NEVER WASH MY
   FEET ! "

   JOHN 13:8

   _____

SAMUEL THE SERPENT

PONTIUS PILATE THE THIEF

JOHN THE BAPTIST NICODEMUS

PETER BARTIMAEUS

JOHN DELILAH

MARK REBEKAH

WHO SAID?

MATCH THE NAMES ON THE FOLLOWING
PAGE TO THE SAYINGS BELOW.

1. "I WILL GIVE HALF OF MY MONEY TO THE
POOR. IF I HAVE CHEATED ANYONE, I
WILL PAY THAT PERSON BACK FOUR
TIMES MORE!"

LUKE 19: 8

_____

2. "A MAN HAS TOLD ME EVERYTHING I HAVE
EVER DONE. COME SEE HIM. MAYBE HE IS
THE CHRIST."

JOHN 4:5-29

_____

3. "I HAVE SINNED AGAINST THE LORD."

2 SAMUEL 12: 13

_____

4. "I SINNED. I GAVE YOU AN INNOCENT
MAN TO KILL."

MATTHEW 27:3-4

_____

5. "COME FOLLOW ME. I WILL MAKE YOU
FISHERMEN FOR ME."

MATTHEW 4:18-19

_____

6. "BUT MAYBE YOU DON'T WANT TO SERVE
THE LORD. YOU MUST CHOOSE FOR
YOURSELVES TODAY. YOU MUST DECIDE
WHOM YOU WILL SERVE."

JOSHUA 24:2-15

_____

179

LUKE

DAVID

PETER

JESUS

JOSHUA

JUDAS
    ISCARIOT

SAMUEL

MATTHEW

ZACCHAEUS

JOHN

ABRAHAM

THE SAMARITAN
    WOMAN

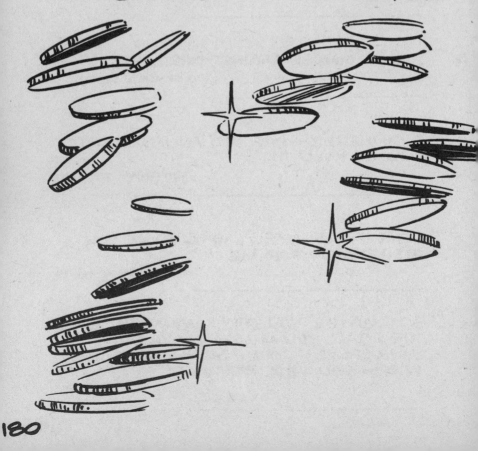

MULTIPLE CHOICE

CIRCLE THE CORRECT ANSWER.
WHO WAS JESUS SPEAKING TO
WHEN HE SAID THE FOLLOWING?

1. " HURRY, COME DOWN. I MUST STAY AT
   YOUR HOUSE TODAY."

   LUKE 19:5

   A. ANDREW

   B. ZACHARIAS

   C. ZACCHAEUS

2. " BEFORE THE ROOSTER CROWS TONIGHT,
   YOU WILL SAY THREE TIMES THAT YOU
   DON'T KNOW ME."

   LUKE 22:61

   A. PETER

   B. LUKE

   C. JUDAS

3. " MARY HAS CHOSEN WHAT IS RIGHT, AND
   IT WILL NEVER BE TAKEN AWAY FROM
   HER."

   LUKE 10:41-42

   A. LAZARUS

   B. MARY MAGDALENE

   C. MARTHA

CONT'D NEXT PAGE...   183

4. " THE ONLY POWER YOU HAVE OVER ME
   IS THE POWER GIVEN TO YOU BY GOD."
   JOHN 19: 10-11

   A. THE SADDUCEES

   B. THE PHARISEES

   C. PONTIUS PILATE

5. " PUT YOUR FINGER HERE. LOOK AT
   MY HANDS. PUT YOUR HAND HERE
   IN MY SIDE. STOP DOUBTING AND
   BELIEVE ."
   JOHN 20: 26-27

   A. THOMAS

   B. PETER

   C. ANDREW

6. " DEAR WOMAN, HERE IS YOUR SON."
   JOHN 19: 26

   A. MARTHA

   B. MARY, JESUS' MOTHER

   C. MARY, WIFE OF CLEOPHAS

MULTIPLE CHOICE

CIRCLE THE CORRECT ANSWER.

WHO WAS THIS WOMAN?

1. THIS WOMAN POURED EXPENSIVE PERFUME ON JESUS' FEET AND WIPED IT OFF WITH HER HAIR.

   JOHN 12:1-3

   A. MARY MAGDALENE

   B. MARY, MARTHA'S SISTER

   C. MARY, JESUS' MOTHER

2. THIS WOMAN WAS THE ONE JESUS FIRST APPEARED TO AFTER HIS RESURRECTION.

   MARK 16:9

   A. MARY MAGDALENE

   B. MARY, WIFE OF CLEOPHAS

   C. MARY, MARTHA'S SISTER

3. THIS WOMAN RECEIVED, FROM JESUS, THE DISCIPLE JOHN TO 'BE HER SON.'

   JOHN 19:25-27

   A. MARY, WIFE OF CLEOPHAS

   B. MARY, JESUS' MOTHER

   C. MARY MAGDALENE

CONT'D NEXT PAGE ...

CONT'D FROM PREVIOUS PAGE.

4. THIS WOMAN HAD SEVEN DEMONS DRIVEN OUT OF HER BY JESUS.

LUKE 8:2

A. MARY MAGDALENE

B. MARY, MARTHA'S SISTER

C. MARY, WIFE OF CLEOPHAS

5. THIS WOMAN WAS SCOLDED FOR NOT HELPING TO MAKE DINNER.

LUKE 10:39-40

A. MARY, WIFE OF CLEOPHAS

B. MARY, JESUS' MOTHER

C. MARY, MARTHA'S SISTER

6. THIS WOMAN'S BROTHER DIED, AND JESUS BROUGHT HIM BACK TO LIFE.

JOHN 11:19-43

A. MARY MAGDALENE

B. MARY, MARTHA'S SISTER

C. MARY, WIFE OF CLEOPHAS

FINISH THE VERSE

TO FIND OUT WHAT THE VERSE BELOW
SAYS, FILL IN THE BLANKS. ALL THE
CONSONANTS ARE THERE. ALL YOU
NEED TO DO IS ADD THE VOWELS.

VOWELS: A E I O U

" MY CH_LD, L_ST_N
  _ND _CC_PT WH_T _
  S_ Y. TH_N Y _ _
  W_ LL H_V_ _ L_NG
  L_F_. _ _M
  G_ _D_NG Y _ _ _N
  W_ SD_ M. _ND _ _M
  L_ _D_NG Y _ _ T_
  D_ WH_T _S
  R_GHT. "

PROVERBS 4:10-11

185

FINISH THE VERSE

TO FIND OUT WHAT THE VERSE BELOW SAYS, FILL IN THE BLANKS. ALL THE CONSONANTS ARE THERE. ALL YOU NEED TO DO IS ADD THE VOWELS.

VOWELS: A E I O U

"MY CH__LD, P__Y __TT__NT____N T__ MY W__RDS. L__ST__N CL__S__LY T__ WH__T __ S__Y. D__N'T __V__R F__RG__T MY W__RDS. K____P TH__M D____P W__TH__N Y____R H____RT."

PROVERBS 4:20-21

UNSCRAMBLE THE VERSE

TO FIND OUT WHAT THE VERSE BELOW SAYS, FILL IN THE BLANKS. ALL THE VOWELS ARE THERE. ALL YOU NEED TO DO IS ADD THE CONSONANTS.

"TEEHS DWROS REA ETH
CREEST OT FLEI OFR SEOHT OHW
NFDI EMHT. EYHT GNRIB HETHAL
TO HET LHWEO DBYO. EB RVEY
FCAULRE TBUOA WAHT UYO HTIKN
ORYU TGSHHTUO RNU UORY FEIL."

"_ _ E _ E _ _ O _ _ _ A _ E _ _ E
_ E _ _ E _ _ O _ I _ E _ O _
_ _ O _ E _ _ O _ I _ _
_ _ E _ . _ _ E _ _ _ I _ _
_ E A _ _ _ _ O _ _ E
_ _ O _ E _ O _ _ . _ E
_ E _ _ _ A _ E _ U _
A _ O U _ _ _ A _ _ O U
_ _ I _ _ . _ O U _
_ _ O U _ _ _ _ _ U _
_ O U _ _ I _ E. "

PROVERBS 4: 22-23

187

UNSCRAMBLE THE VERSE

TO FIND OUT WHAT THE VERSE BELOW SAYS, FILL IN THE BLANKS. ALL THE VOWELS ARE THERE. ALL YOU NEED TO DO IS ADD THE CONSONANTS.

" NTOD SEU RYUO HMTOU OT LTEL SLEI. NDOT VREE AYS GHTSIN TTHA EAR TNO RUTE. KEPE YORU YEES UCESDOF NO WTHA SI ITRHG. EEPK LKNOGOI RGHTTSIA HDEAA OT AWTH SI DGOO. "

" _ O _ ' _   U _ E   _ O U _   _ O U _ _
_ O   _ E _ _   _ I E _ .   _ O _ ' _
E _ E _   _ A _   _ _ I _ _ _
_ _ A _   A _ E   _ O _   _ _ U E.
_ E E _   _ O U _   E _ E _
_ O _ U _ E _   O _   _ _ A _
I _   _ I _ _ _ .   _ E E _
_ O O _ I _ _   _ _ _ A I _ _ _
A _ E A _   _ O   _ _ A _ I _
_ O O _ . "

PROVERBS 4: 24-25

188

TRUE / FALSE

1. JONAH TOLD THE PEOPLE OF NINEVEH THAT THEIR CITY WOULD BE DESTROYED IN FORTY DAYS.

JONAH 3:4

TRUE _____ FALSE _____

2. GOLIATH CHALLENGED THE ISRAELITES THREE TIMES A DAY FOR FORTY DAYS.

1 SAMUEL 17:16

TRUE _____ FALSE _____

3. ABRAHAM'S SERVANT WENT ALL THE WAY TO MESOPOTAMIA TO FIND A WIFE FOR ISAAC.

GENESIS 24:2-10

TRUE _____ FALSE _____

CONT'D NEXT PAGE...

4. DANIEL AND HIS FRIENDS ATE NOTHING BUT MEAT AND VEGETABLES FOR TEN DAYS.

DANIEL 1:12

TRUE _____ FALSE _____

5. WHEN THE RESIDENTS OF NINEVEH REPENTED, THEY PUT SACKCLOTH ON ALL THEIR ANIMALS.

JONAH 3:8

TRUE _____ FALSE _____

6. MORDECAI ACTED LIKE ESTHER'S FATHER, BUT HE WAS REALLY HER COUSIN.

ESTHER 2:7

TRUE _____ FALSE _____

TRUE / FALSE

1. LAZARUS HAD BEEN IN THE TOMB FOR THREE DAYS BEFORE JESUS CALLED HIM OUT.

   JOHN 11:39

   TRUE _____ FALSE _____

2. JOSEPH WAS TWENTY-THREE YEARS OLD WHEN HIS BROTHERS SOLD HIM TO THE ISHMAELITES.

   GENESIS 37:2

   TRUE _____ FALSE _____

3. BEFORE HIS MINISTRY, JESUS WAS A CARPENTER.

   MARK 6:3

   TRUE _____ FALSE _____

CONT'D NEXT PAGE ...

4. AFTER MOSES WAS GIVEN THE TEN COMMANDMENTS, HE WORE A VEIL OVER HIS GLOWING FACE.

EXODUS 34:33-35

TRUE _____ FALSE _____

5. THE LEVITES HAD TO RETIRE AT THE AGE OF SIXTY-FIVE.

NUMBERS 8:23-25

TRUE _____ FALSE _____

6. AFTER SAUL KILLED HIMSELF, THE PHILISTINES CUT OFF HIS HEAD AND HUNG IT IN A TEMPLE.

1 CHRONICLES 10:8-10

TRUE _____ FALSE _____

192

MULTIPLE CHOICE

CIRCLE THE CORRECT ANSWER.

1. WHAT WERE THE LAST WORDS JESUS SPOKE ON THE CROSS?

   JOHN 19:30

   A. "I AM THIRSTY."

   B. "FATHER, FORGIVE THEM."

   C. "IT IS FINISHED."

2. WHEN JOSEPH BURIED JESUS, WHO WAS WITH HIM?

   JOHN 19:38-39

   A. JOHN

   B. NICODEMUS

   C. JESUS' MOTHER

3. JESUS WAS KNOWN AS A...?

   MATTHEW 2:23

   A. NAZARENE

   B. ISRAELITE

   C. ROMAN

CONT'D NEXT PAGE...

4. WHAT DOES "EMMANUEL" MEAN ?

MATTHEW 1:23

   A. JESUS WITH US

   B. GOD WITH US

   C. FATHER WITH US

5. WHO STAYED WITH NAOMI RATHER THAN RETURN TO HER OWN PEOPLE ?

RUTH 1:16-19

   A. ORPAH

   B. MOAB

   C. RUTH

6. WHERE WILL YOU FIND THE BOOK OF GALATIANS ?

   A. THE OLD TESTAMENT

   B. THE NEW TESTAMENT

   C. THE DICTIONARY

MULTIPLE CHOICE
CIRCLE THE CORRECT ANSWER

1. WHO WAS ON TRIAL AT THE SAME TIME
   AS JESUS ?

   MATTHEW 27:15-18

   A. BARABBAS

   B. JUDA

   C. PHARISEES

2. WHERE DID THE DEMONS BEG JESUS
   TO ALLOW THEM TO GO AFTER THEY WERE
   CAST OUT OF THE TWO MEN ?

   MATTHEW 8:32

   A. A HERD OF SHEEP

   B. A HERD OF COWS

   C. A HERD OF PIGS

3. AFTER JESUS HEALED THE TWO BLIND
   MEN, HE TOLD THEM TO ...?

   MATTHEW 9:30

   A. BE SILENT ABOUT IT.

   B. GO TELL THE PHARISEES.

   C. GO WASH THEIR FACES.

CONT'D NEXT PAGE ...

195

4. WHO DIVIDED THE JORDAN RIVER
WITH HIS CLOAK ?

2 KINGS 2:8

    A. JOSHUA

    B. ELIJAH

    C. DANIEL

5. WHO BUILT A CALF OF GOLD TO MAKE
THE ISRAELITES HAPPY ?

EXODUS 32:1-4

    A. MOSES

    B. AARON

    C. JONAH

6. WHAT WAS ANDREW'S OCCUPATION
BEFORE HE WAS CALLED BY JESUS ?

MATTHEW 4:18

    A. A CARPENTER

    B. A TAX COLLECTOR

    C. A FISHERMAN

196

WHO WAS HIS MOTHER?

MATCH MOTHER TO SON BY
DRAWING A LINE FROM ONE
NAME TO ANOTHER.

HAGGITH   JOSEPH
    1 KINGS 1:5

RACHEL   AHAZIAH
    GENESIS 30: 22-24

AHINOAM   ADONIJAH
    1 SAMUEL 14: 49-50

ATHALIAH   JUDAH
    2 KINGS 8: 26

LEAH   JONATHAN
    GENESIS 29: 32-35

GOO-- GOO-- GOOO...

197

MULTIPLE CHOICE
CIRCLE THE CORRECT ANSWER.

1. HOW MANY YEARS DID SAMSON JUDGE ISRAEL?

   JUDGES 16:31

   A. FIVE YEARS

   B. TWENTY YEARS

   C. FIFTEEN YEARS

2. WHAT HAPPENED TO THE SOLDIERS WHEN THEY SAW THE ANGEL AT THE TOMB?

   MATTHEW 28:2-4

   A. THEY RAN.

   B. THEY SANG.

   C. THEY BECAME LIKE DEAD MEN.

3. WHAT IS THE TWENTY-FIFTH BOOK OF THE NEW TESTAMENT?

   A. 1 JOHN

   B. REVELATION

   C. 3 JOHN

CONT'D NEXT PAGE ...

4. WHAT WAS CORNELIUS' OCCUPATION?

ACTS 10:1

    A. A COOK

    B. A TENTMAKER

    C. A CENTURION

5. PAUL SAID, "YOU ARE ALL THE CHILDREN OF GOD BY..."

GALATIANS 3:26

    A. "GETTING BAPTIZED."

    B. "FAITH IN JESUS CHRIST."

    C. "GOING TO CHURCH."

6. WHAT MAN CALLED HIMSELF A VOICE CRYING OUT IN THE WILDERNESS?

MARK 1:2-8

    A. ELIJAH

    B. JOHN THE BAPTIST

    C. JOHN

199

Answer Pages

USING THE WORD LIST BELOW, FILL IN THE BLANKS TO COMPLETE THE VERSES.

"_HAPPY_ IS THE PERSON WHO DOESN'T _LISTEN_ TO THE WICKED. HE DOESN'T GO WHERE _SINNERS_ GO. HE DOESN'T DO WHAT _BAD_ PEOPLE DO. HE LOVES THE _LORD'S_ TEACHINGS. HE THINKS ABOUT THOSE _TEACHINGS_ _DAY_ AND _NIGHT_."

— PSALM 1:1-2

WORD LIST	
TEACHINGS	LISTEN
BAD	DAY
NIGHT	SINNERS
HAPPY	LORD'S

1

HOW MUCH OF THE BIBLE DO YOU KNOW?

MATCH THE ANSWERS ON THE FOLLOWING PAGE TO THE QUESTIONS BELOW.

1. WHO SAID, "I AM WHO I AM"?
   GOD — ROMANS 3:14

2. WHAT DID GOD CREATE ON THE FIRST DAY?
   LIGHT — GENESIS 1:3

3. WHO BUILT THE ARK?
   NOAH — GENESIS 6:13-14

4. HOW MANY SONS DID NOAH HAVE?
   THREE — GENESIS 6:10

5. WHAT WERE THE NAMES OF NOAH'S SONS?
   HAM _SHEM_ _JAPHETH_

6. WHO SAID, "AM I SUPPOSED TO TAKE CARE OF MY BROTHER?"
   CAIN — GENESIS 4:9

2

MULTIPLE CHOICE

CIRCLE THE CORRECT ANSWER

1. WHOSE LIFE WAS SAVED BY BEING LOWERED OVER A WALL IN A BASKET? — ACTS 9:25
   A. JOHN'S
   B. THE CRIPPLED MAN
   C. SAUL'S ✓

2. DAVID SAID THAT GOD MADE MAN A LITTLE LOWER THAN WHOM? — PSALM 8
   A. STARS
   B. ANGELS ✓
   C. ANIMALS

3. WHERE WAS MOSES STANDING WHEN GOD TOLD HIM TO TAKE OFF HIS SHOES? — EXODUS 3:5
   A. ON A MOUNTAIN
   B. ON HOLY GROUND ✓
   C. ON A BEACH

4

CON'T FROM PREVIOUS PAGE.

4. HOW MANY DISCIPLES HAD THE NAME OF JAMES? — MATTHEW 10:2-3
   A. TWO ✓
   B. FOUR
   C. SEVEN

5. WHAT DOES THE HEBREW WORD "ABBA," MEAN? — ROMANS 8:15
   A. HELLO
   B. DADDY ✓
   C. MOMMY

6. WHO DID JESUS SAY THE SABBATH WAS MADE FOR? — MARK 2:27
   A. GOD
   B. UNBELIEVERS
   C. MAN ✓

5

MATCH THE ANSWERS

MATCH THE ANSWERS ON THE FOLLOWING PAGE TO THE QUESTIONS BELOW.

1. WHO ASKED GOD TO SPARE SODOM?
   ABRAHAM — GENESIS 18:23-33

2. WHO WROTE FIRST AND SECOND CORINTHIANS?
   PAUL — 1 COR. 1:1 ; 2 COR. 1:1

3. WHO DID JESUS SAY WILL INHERIT THE EARTH?
   THE MEEK — MATTHEW 5:5

4. WHAT IS THE NAME GIVEN TO JESUS THAT MEANS "GOD IS WITH US"?
   EMMANUEL — MATTHEW 1:23

5. WHAT WILL GOD GIVE US PLENTY OF IF WE ASK HIM?
   WISDOM — JAMES 1:5

6. WHERE IN EGYPT DID JOSEPH'S FAMILY LIVE?
   GOSHEN — GENESIS 47:6

6

MULTIPLE CHOICE

CIRCLE THE CORRECT ANSWER.

1. WHAT WAS SARAH'S NAME BEFORE GOD CHANGED IT? — GENESIS 17:15
   A. SALLY
   B. HAGAR
   C. SARAI ✓

2. WHO DID PAUL CALL HIS OWN SON? — 1 TIMOTHY 1:2
   A. PETER
   B. TIMOTHY ✓
   C. JOHN

3. WHO PREACHED ON THE DAY OF PENTECOST? — ACTS 2:14
   A. JOHN
   B. PAUL
   C. PETER ✓

8

...cont'd from previous page

4. WHAT DID JACOB WEAR TO TRICK HIS
FATHER? *Genesis 27:16-24*

   A. SHEEPSKIN
   B. BEARSKIN
   C. GOATSKIN

5. HOW MANY PLAGUES DID GOD BRING
ON EGYPT? *Exodus 7-11*

   A. SEVEN
   B. TEN
   C. TWELVE

6. WHAT WAS THE NAME OF THE WELL THAT
THE SAMARITAN WOMAN DREW WATER
FROM? *John 4:7*

   A. SAMARIA WELL
   B. JOSEPH'S WELL
   C. JACOB'S WELL

9

FILL IN THE BLANKS

WORD LIST		
LIFE	RESURRECTION	
FOOL	WICKED	
LORD	SHEPHERD	
EVERYTHING	NEED	

1. IN JOHN 11:25, JESUS SAID, "I AM
THE RESURRECTION
AND THE LIFE."

2. IN PSALM 14:1, IT SAYS, "A
WICKED FOOL SAYS
TO HIMSELF, 'THERE IS NO GOD'."

3. IN PSALM 23:1, IT SAYS, "THE
LORD IS MY SHEPHERD.
I HAVE EVERYTHING
I NEED."

10

FILL IN THE BLANKS

WORD LIST		
LIGHT	CREATED	FEMALE
SAVES	IMAGE	
PROTECTS	AFRAID	
WAY	TRUTH	
LIFE	MALE	

1. IN PSALM 27:1, IT SAYS, "THE LORD
IS MY LIGHT AND THE
ONE WHO SAVES ME. I
FEAR NO ONE. THE LORD
PROTECTS MY LIFE.
I AM AFRAID OF NO ONE."

2. IN JOHN 14:6, JESUS SAID, "I AM THE
WAY. I AM THE TRUTH
AND THE LIFE."

3. IN GENESIS 1:27, IT SAYS, "SO GOD
CREATED HUMAN BEINGS IN
HIS IMAGE. IN THE IMAGE OF
GOD HE CREATED THEM. HE CREATED
THEM MALE AND FEMALE."

11

MATCH THE ANSWERS
MATCH THE ANSWERS ON THE
FOLLOWING PAGE TO THE QUESTIONS
BELOW.

1. WHO WAS ISHMAEL'S MOTHER?
HAGAR *Genesis 16:15*

2. WHO WAS THE FATHER OF MANY NATIONS?
ABRAHAM *Genesis 17:1-8*

3. WHO WAS THE BROTHER OF MARTHA
AND MARY? *John 11:1-2*
LAZARUS

4. WHAT IS THE ROOT OF ALL EVIL? *1 Timothy 6:10*
LOVE OF MONEY

5. WHAT IS THE JEWISH DAY OF REST
CALLED? *Exodus 20:10*
SABBATH

6. IN WHAT AREA IS BETHLEHEM
LOCATED? *Matthew 2:1*
JUDEA

12

MULTIPLE CHOICE
CIRCLE THE CORRECT ANSWER

1. WHAT WAS THE NAME OF ABRAHAM'S
PROMISED SON? *Genesis 21:3*

   A. ISHMAEL
   B. RONALD
   C. ISAAC

2. WHAT WAS THE NAME OF JACOB'S
YOUNGEST SON? *Genesis 35:18*

   A. JOSEPH
   B. JUDAH
   C. BENJAMIN

3. WHO DID AQUILA AND PRISCILLA MEET
IN CORINTH? *Acts 18:1-2*

   A. JOHN
   B. PAUL
   C. PETER

cont'd on next page.

14

...cont'd from previous page

4. WHAT DID KING BELSHAZZAR SEE ON
THE WALL? *Daniel 5:1-8*

   A. FINGERPRINTS
   B. A HAND WRITING
   C. A BUG

5. WHAT DID GOD MAKE GROW OVER JONAH
TO GIVE HIM SHADE? *Jonah 4:6*

   A. A HOUSE
   B. A TREE
   C. A VINE

6. WHERE DID KING SOLOMON FIND
CEDAR TREES FOR THE TEMPLE? *1 Kings 5:6*

   A. A LUMBER YARD
   B. HIS BACK YARD
   C. LEBANON

15

MULTIPLE CHOICE
CIRCLE THE CORRECT ANSWER

1. HOW MANY BOOKS ARE THERE IN THE
BIBLE?

   A. SIXTY-EIGHT
   B. SIXTY-SIX
   C. THIRTY-FOUR

2. WHAT COMMANDMENT SAYS, "YOU
MUST NOT MURDER ANYONE"? *Exodus 20:13*

   A. TWELFTH
   B. SIXTH
   C. SEVENTH

3. HOW MANY BOOKS ARE IN THE
NEW TESTAMENT?

   A. TWENTY-SIX
   B. TWENTY-EIGHT
   C. TWENTY-SEVEN

cont'd on next page.

16

...cont'd from previous page

4. HOW MANY FRIENDS CAME TO SPEAK
WITH JOB? *Job 2:11*

   A. ONE
   B. THREE
   C. THIRTY-SIX

5. ON WHICH DAY DID GOD CREATE THE
SUN, MOON, AND STARS? *Genesis 1:14-19*

   A. SECOND
   B. FOURTH
   C. SIXTH

6. HOW MANY TIMES DID JESUS ASK
PETER IF HE LOVED HIM? *John 21:15-17*

   A. ONE
   B. THREE
   C. FIVE

17

FILL IN THE BLANKS

WORD LIST		
PATIENT	TRUST	ANGRY
JEALOUS	RUDE	HOPES
TRUTH	SELFISH	WRONGS
BRAG	STRONG	HAPPY
PROUD	KIND	

"LOVE IS PATIENT AND
KIND. LOVE IS NOT JEALOUS.
IT DOES NOT BRAG, AND IT IS NOT
PROUD. LOVE IS NOT RUDE.
IT IS NOT SELFISH, AND
DOES NOT BECOME ANGRY
EASILY. LOVE DOES NOT REMEMBER
WRONGS DONE AGAINST IT.
LOVE IS NOT HAPPY WITH
EVIL, BUT IS HAPPY WITH
TRUTH.

cont'd next page...

18

...cont'd from previous page.

LOVE PATIENTLY ACCEPTS ALL THINGS.
IT ALWAYS **TRUSTS**, ALWAYS
HOPES, AND ALWAYS
CONTINUES **STRONG** "

1 CORINTHIANS 13: 4-7

THIS IS LOVE

19

MATCH THE ANSWERS
MATCH THE ANSWERS ON THE FOLLOWING
PAGE TO THE QUESTIONS BELOW.

1. WHO SENT HIS SONS TO EGYPT TO
BUY GRAIN ?   GENESIS 42: 1-3
JACOB

2. WHO SAID TO JESUS, "YOU ARE THE CHRIST,
THE SON OF THE LIVING GOD "?
MATTHEW 16: 16
PETER

3. WHO SAID, "WHEN I NEEDED CLOTHES,
YOU CLOTHED ME "?   MATTHEW 25: 36
JESUS

4. HOW MANY BOOKS IN THE BIBLE ARE
NAMED " JOHN " ?
FOUR

5. ON WHICH DAY DID GOD CREATE THE
ANIMALS OF THE WATER AND THE AIR ?
GENESIS 1: 20-23
FIFTH

6. WHAT ARE THE STORIES CALLED THAT
JESUS TAUGHT BY ?   MATTHEW 13: 3
PARABLES

20

MATCH THE ANSWERS
MATCH THE ANSWERS ON THE FOLLOWING
PAGE TO THE QUESTIONS BELOW.

1. WHO SOLD HIS BIRTHRIGHT ?
ESAU   GENESIS 25: 29-34

2. WHO WAS JACOB TRICKED INTO
MARRYING ?   GENESIS 29: 23-25
LEAH

3. WHAT OLD TESTAMENT COUPLE HAD
TWIN SONS ?   GENESIS 25: 20-26
ISAAC & REBEKAH

4. WHOSE DAUGHTER DANCED AT HEROD'S
BIRTHDAY PARTY ?   MATTHEW 14:6
HERODIAS'

5. WHAT DID SOLOMON HAVE SEVEN
HUNDRED OF ?   1 KINGS 11:3
WIVES

6. ON THE ROAD TO WHAT CITY DID THE GOOD
SAMARITAN HELP THE BEATEN MAN ?
JERICHO   LUKE 10: 30-35

22

MULTIPLE CHOICE
CIRCLE THE CORRECT ANSWER

1. WHO WAS MOSES' WIFE ?
   A. HAGAR   EXODUS 2:21
   B. ZIPPORAH
   C. REBEKAH

2. WHO WAS THE FIRST PRIEST OF ISRAEL ?
   A. ABRAHAM   EXODUS 28: 1
   B. MOSES
   C. AARON

3. WHO WAS A JUDGE FOR THE PEOPLE OF
ISRAEL FOR TWENTY YEARS ?
   A. SAUL   JUDGES 16: 31
   B. SAMSON
   C. DAVID

CONT'D NEXT PAGE...

24

...cont'd from previous page

4. WHO PREACHED IN THE WILDERNESS OF
JUDEA ?   MATTHEW 3:1
   A. JOHN
   B. JESUS
   C. JOHN THE BAPTIST

5. WHAT WAS THE NAME OF MARY'S SISTER
WHO WORKED HARD IN THE KITCHEN ?
LUKE 10:40
   A. RUTH
   B. DEBORAH
   C. MARTHA

6. WHO WROTE THE BOOK OF REVELATION ?
REVELATION 1:4
   A. PAUL
   B. JOHN
   C. PETER

25

MATCH THE ANSWERS
MATCH THE ANSWERS ON THE FOLLOWING
PAGE TO THE QUESTIONS BELOW.

1. HOW OLD WAS ABRAHAM WHEN ISAAC
WAS BORN ?   GENESIS 21: 5
ONE HUNDRED

2. HOW MANY DAYS WAS SAUL BLIND ?
THREE   ACTS 9:9

3. WHAT COMMANDMENT IS " HONOR YOUR
FATHER AND YOUR MOTHER " ?
EXODUS 20: 12
FIFTH

4. WHAT DOES " GENESIS " MEAN ?
BEGINNING

5. WHAT LANGUAGE WAS THE NEW
TESTAMENT WRITTEN IN ?
GREEK

6. WHAT NEW TESTAMENT BOOK TELLS
OF JESUS GOING UP TO HEAVEN ?
ACTS

26

FILL IN THE BLANKS

WORD LIST	
STAND	POOR
KNOCK	ANYONE
VOICE	OPENS
EAT	HE

"HERE I AM! I **STAND** AT
THE **POOR** AND **KNOCK**.
IF **ANYONE** HEARS MY
VOICE AND **OPENS**
THE DOOR, I WILL COME IN AND
EAT WITH HIM, AND **HE**
WILL EAT WITH ME."
REVELATION 3:20

28

FILL IN THE BLANKS

WORD LIST	
ASK	KNOCK
SEARCH	OPEN
FIND	GOD
YOU	POOR

"CONTINUE TO **ASK** AND **GOD**
WILL GIVE TO YOU. CONTINUE TO
SEARCH AND **YOU**
WILL **FIND** CONTINUE TO
KNOCK AND THE **DOOR**
WILL BE **OPEN** FOR YOU."
MATTHEW 7:7

29

MULTIPLE CHOICE
CIRCLE THE CORRECT ANSWER

1. WHO WAS TAKEN OUT OF SODOM BEFORE
IT WAS DESTROYED ?   GENESIS 19: 15-16
   A. ABRAHAM AND HIS FAMILY
   B. LOT AND HIS FAMILY
   C. ISAAC AND HIS FAMILY

2. WHO WAS ISAAC'S FATHER ?
   A. JACOB   GENESIS 21:3
   B. NOAH
   C. ABRAHAM

3. WHO WAS SARAI'S MAID ?
   A. REBEKAH   GENESIS 16:1
   B. HAGAR
   C. RUTH

CONT'D NEXT PAGE

30

cont'd from previous page

2. JESUS RAISED LAZARUS FROM THE DEAD. WHO WERE LAZARUS' SISTERS?

A. MARY AND ELIZABETH

B. RUTH AND NAOMI

C. MARTHA AND MARY

3. WHAT DID JESUS SAY HE WOULD BUILD HIS CHURCH ON? *Matthew 16:18*

A. THIS MOUNTAIN

B. THIS HILL

C. THIS ROCK

4. WHAT DID JUDAS DO AFTER HE BETRAYED JESUS? *Matthew 27:5*

A. SAID SORRY

B. CRIED

C. HANGED HIMSELF

31

MULTIPLE CHOICE
CIRCLE THE CORRECT ANSWER.

1. WHAT DOES TESTAMENT MEAN?

A. TO TEST

B. AGREEMENT

C. BOOKS

2. WHAT DID THE ISRAELITES PUT ON THEIR DOOR POSTS SO THAT THE DEATH ANGEL WOULD PASS BY? *Exodus 12:21-28*

A. GOAT'S BLOOD

B. PAINT

C. LAMB'S BLOOD

3. WHAT ARE WE TO POUR ON THE SICK SO THAT THE PRAYER OF FAITH WILL MAKE THEM WELL? *James 5:14*

A. MEDICINE

B. WATER

C. OIL

cont'd next page.

32

---

cont'd from previous page

4. WHAT ARE WE SUPPOSED TO DO WHEN WE SIN? *James 5:16*

A. FORGET ABOUT IT

B. CONFESS IT TO EACH OTHER

C. PRETEND IT DIDN'T HAPPEN

5. JESUS CALLED MATTHEW TO BE A DISCIPLE. WHAT WAS HIS JOB BEFORE JESUS CALLED HIM? *Matthew 9:9*

A. A FISHERMAN

B. A TAX COLLECTOR

C. A BASEBALL PLAYER

6. WHAT DID JESUS SAY HE WOULD MAKE PETER AND ANDREW? *Mark 1:16-17*

A. SINGERS

B. KINGS

C. FISHERS OF MEN

33

MATCH THE ANSWERS
MATCH THE ANSWERS ON THE FOLLOWING PAGE TO THE QUESTIONS BELOW.

1. IN THE ARMOR OF GOD, WHAT IS THE SHIELD CALLED? *Ephesians 6:16*

FAITH

2. WHAT IS THE HELMET CALLED? *Ephesians 6:17*

SALVATION

3. WHAT IS THE SWORD CALLED? *Ephesians 6:17*

WORD OF GOD

4. WHAT IS THE BELT CALLED? *Ephesians 6:14*

TRUTH

5. WHAT INGREDIENT IN THE KITCHEN DID JESUS SAY WE WERE LIKE? *Matthew 5:13*

SALT

6. WHAT BOOK OF THE BIBLE HAS THE MOST CHAPTERS?

PSALMS

34

MATCH THE ANSWERS
MATCH THE ANSWERS ON THE FOLLOWING PAGE TO THE QUESTIONS BELOW.

1. IN THE DESERT, GOD GAVE THE ISRAELITES MANNA TO EAT. WHAT ELSE DID GOD GIVE THEM?

QUAILS

2. WHAT DOES JESUS GIVE TO THOSE WHO CHOOSE TO FOLLOW HIM? *John 10:27-28*

ETERNAL LIFE

3. WHAT SPECIAL DAY WAS IT WHEN THE BELIEVERS RECEIVED THE HOLY SPIRIT? *Acts 2:1-4*

PENTECOST

4. A MAN REAPS WHAT HE ... WHAT? *Galatians 6:7*

SOWS

5. WHAT DID JESUS SAY HE HAD OVERCOME? *John 16:33*

WORLD

6. IN WHAT COUNTRY DID ISAAC FIND A WIFE? *Genesis 24:10*

MESOPOTAMIA

36

FILL IN THE BLANKS

WORD LIST	
PERSON	JESUS
LIVE	BREAD
EATING	BY
EVERYTHING	LORD

JESUS SAID, " A **PERSON** DOES NOT **LIVE** ONLY BY **EATING BREAD**, BUT A PERSON LIVES **BY EVERYTHING** THE **LORD** SAYS." *Matthew 4:4*

38

FILL IN THE BLANKS

WORD LIST	
BEGINS	RESPECT
WISDOM	LORD
KNOWLEDGE	FOOLISH
SELF-CONTROL	

KNOWLEDGE BEGINS WITH **RESPECT** FOR THE **LORD**, BUT **FOOLISH** PEOPLE HATE **WISDOM** AND **SELF-CONTROL**. *Proverbs 1:7*

39

FILL IN THE BLANKS

WORD LIST	
LOVE	KINDNESS
JOY	FAITHFULNESS
SELF-CONTROL	PEACE
GENTLENESS	PATIENCE
GOODNESS	

" BUT THE SPIRIT GIVES **LOVE**, **JOY**, **PEACE**, **PATIENCE**, **KINDNESS**, **GOODNESS**, **FAITHFULNESS**, **GENTLENESS** AND **SELF-CONTROL**. THERE IS NO LAW THAT SAYS THESE THINGS ARE WRONG. " *Galatians 5:22-23*

40

FILL IN THE BLANKS

WORD LIST	
HELPER	EVERYTHING
NAME	YOU
HOLY	REMEMBER
FATHER	ME

" BUT THE **HELPER** WILL TEACH YOU **EVERYTHING**. HE WILL CAUSE YOU TO **REMEMBER** ALL THE THINGS I TOLD **YOU**. THIS HELPER IS THE **HOLY** SPIRIT WHOM THE **FATHER** WILL SEND IN MY **NAME**. " *John 14:26*

41

Match the answers in the following page to the questions below.

1. In the parable of the talents, how many servants were given talents? **THREE**
2. How old was Jairus' daughter when she got sick? **TWELVE**
3. How many wineskins, or "wods", did Jesus give to the Pharisees? **EIGHT**
4. How many wives did Jacob have? **FOUR**
5. How many pieces of silver was Judas paid to betray Jesus? **THIRTY**
6. How many concubines did King Solomon have? **THREE HUNDRED**

42

MATCH THE ANSWERS
Match the answers in the following page to the questions below.

1. How many were at the Last Supper with Jesus? **TWELVE**
2. How long is a millennium? **ONE THOUSAND YEARS**
3. Which Old Testament book tells about the life of Abraham? **GENESIS**
4. What people fought to know the secret of Samson's strength? **PHILISTINES**
5. Who was the only female judge of Israel? **DEBORAH**
6. The Lord said He is the Alpha and the Omega. What does Omega mean? **LAST, END**

44

MULTIPLE CHOICE
Circle the correct answer.

1. Who was Joseph's mother?
   A. Leah
   (B.) Rachel
   C. Rebekah
2. Who was the first king of Israel?
   A. Aaron
   B. ?
   (C.) Saul
3. What was Belshazzar's other name?
   A. Simon
   (B.) Daniel
   C. Job

cont'd next page...

46

...cont'd from previous page.

4. Who was the cousin of Mordecai that became a queen?
   A. Ruth
   B. Naomi
   (C.) Esther
5. Who wrote the riddle about the lion?
   A. Judges
   B. Solomon
   (C.) Samson
6. Who called down fire from heaven?
   A. Elisha
   (B.) Elijah
   C. ?

47

MULTIPLE CHOICE
Circle the correct answer.

1. What excuse did Aaron give to God for why he didn't want to go to Egypt?
   A. "I'm too tired."
   B. "I have other plans."
   (C.) "I am slow to speak."
2. What did Joseph interpret for Pharaoh?
   A. his wife's dreams
   B. a recipe for pudding
   (C.) his dreams
3. Jesus said that when He returns again, He will come like a ...what?
   A. flash of lightning
   B. day of thunder
   (C.) thief in the night

cont'd next page...

48

...cont'd from previous page.

4. What did the women bring to Jesus' tomb?
   A. flowers
   (B.) sweet spices
   C. people
5. What did Noah do for a living?
   A. farm
   B. build
   (C.) hunt
6. In the parable of the sower, what does the seed stand for?
   A. a plant
   B. corn
   (C.) the word of God

49

MULTIPLE CHOICE
Circle the correct answer.

1. What did Jesus tell the disciples to do if they were not welcome at someone's home?
   A. get angry
   B. whine and cry
   (C.) shake the dust off your feet
2. What was John the Baptist's clothing made of?
   A. silk
   B. wool
   (C.) camel's hair
3. What kind of crown will Jesus give us if we are faithful to the end?
   A. crown of gold
   B. crown of silver
   (C.) crown of life

cont'd next page...

50

...cont'd from previous page.

4. What are we told to take up to follow Jesus?
   A. our suitcase
   (B.) our crosses
   C. our coats
5. Faith without what is dead?
   A. works
   (B.) works
   C. wisdom
6. What did Daniel and his friends refuse to eat and drink at the king's table?
   A. liver, onions and candied yams
   (B.) meat and wine
   C. pizza and soda

51

FILL IN THE BLANKS

WORD LIST	
TRUST	EVERYTHING
SUCCESS	OWN
HEART	REMEMBER
DEPEND	LORD

"**TRUST** in the **LORD** with all your **HEART**. Don't **DEPEND** on your **OWN** understanding. **REMEMBER** the Lord in **EVERYTHING** you do. And He will give you **SUCCESS**!"

52

FILL IN THE BLANKS

WORD LIST
DEPEND	SUN
NOONDAY	LORD
FAIRNESS	GOODNESS
HE	CARE

• _DEPEND_ on the _LORD_, TRUST HIM AND _HE_ WILL TAKE _CARE_ OF YOU. THEN YOUR _GOODNESS_ WILL SHINE LIKE THE _SUN_. YOUR _FAIRNESS_ WILL SHINE LIKE THE _NOONDAY_ SUN."

PSALM 37:5-6

53

FILL IN THE BLANKS

WORD LIST
WAIT	LEADS
TRUST	RICH
LORD	ANGRY
UPSET	TROUBLE

• _WAIT_ AND _TRUST_ THE _LORD_. DON'T BE _UPSET_ WHEN OTHERS GET _RICH_ OR WHEN SOMEONE ELSE'S PLANS SUCCEED. DON'T GET _ANGRY_. DON'T BE UPSET; IT ONLY _LEADS_ TO _TROUBLE_."

PSALM 37:7-8

54

FILL IN THE BLANKS

WORD LIST
EAT	ROARING
CAREFUL	CONTROL
DEVIL	LOOKING
HE	ENEMY

• _CONTROL_ YOURSELVES AND BE _CAREFUL_. THE _DEVIL_ IS YOUR _ENEMY_. AND _HE_ GOES AROUND LIKE A _ROARING_ LION _LOOKING_ FOR SOMEONE TO _EAT_."

1 PETER 5:8

YUM! YUM!

55

MATCH THE ANSWERS

MATCH THE ANSWERS ON THE FOLLOWING PAGE TO THE QUESTIONS BELOW.

1. WHO DID ISAAC BLESS INSTEAD OF ESAU?
   JACOB GENESIS 27:26-29

2. WHO TOLD THE BROTHERS OF JOSEPH NOT TO HARM JOSEPH?
   REUBEN GENESIS 37:22

3. WHO SAID THEY SHOULD SELL JOSEPH RATHER THAN KILL HIM?
   JUDAH GENESIS 37:26-27

4. WHO HAD A DREAM ABOUT THE SUN, MOON, AND STARS BOWING DOWN TO HIM?
   JOSEPH GENESIS 37:9-11

5. WHO PURCHASED JOSEPH AS A SLAVE?
   POTIPHAR GENESIS 37:36

6. WHO WAS JOSEPH'S MOTHER?
   RACHEL GENESIS 30:22-24

56

MATCH THE ANSWERS

MATCH THE ANSWERS ON THE FOLLOWING PAGE TO THE QUESTIONS BELOW.

1. WHO WAS THE FATHER OF JAMES AND JOHN?
   ZEBEDEE MARK 3:10

2. WHAT TWO DISCIPLES FOLLOWED JESUS FIRST?
   SIMON PETER & ANDREW MATTHEW 4:18

3. HOW MANY BOOKS IN THE NEW TESTAMENT HAVE ONLY ONE CHAPTER?
   FOUR

4. THE FOUR GOSPELS ARE ABOUT WHOM?
   JESUS

5. WHAT DO WE CALL THE DAY IN WHICH WE REMEMBER JESUS' DEATH ON THE CROSS?
   GOOD FRIDAY

6. WHICH DISCIPLE WAS SENT TO THE ISLAND OF PATMOS?
   JOHN REVELATION 1:9

58

MULTIPLE CHOICE

CIRCLE THE CORRECT ANSWER.

1. ON WHAT WAS JOHN THE BAPTIST'S HEAD PUT TO GIVE TO HERODIAS' DAUGHTER? MATTHEW 14:8
   A. STICK
   B. PLATTER
   C. BOWL

2. WHAT HAPPENED TO THE MEN THAT THREW SHADRACH, MESHACH, AND ABEDNEGO INTO THE FIERY FURNACE? DANIEL 3:22
   A. THEIR HAIR WAS SINGED
   B. THE HEAT OF THE FIRE KILLED THEM.
   C. THEY GOT VERY WARM

3. WHAT DOES JAMES SAY SHALL SAVE THE SICK? JAMES 5:15
   A. A DOCTOR
   B. GOING TO THE HOSPITAL
   C. A PRAYER OF FAITH

60

CONT'D FROM PREVIOUS PAGE.

4. WHAT WAS JOHN THE BAPTIST UNWORTHY TO UNTIE? MARK 1:7
   A. JESUS' NECKTIE
   B. JESUS' CLOAK
   C. JESUS' SANDALS

5. WHY DID MARY AND JOSEPH GO TO BETHLEHEM? LUKE 2:1-4
   A. FOR A VACATION
   B. TO REGISTER THEIR NAMES & TO PAY TAXES
   C. TO VISIT ELIZABETH

6. WHAT HAPPENED TO THE WATERS OF JORDAN WHEN MOSES THREW A TREE IN? EXODUS 15:25-26
   A. THE TREE BLOCKED THE WATER.
   B. MADE THE WATER SWEET OR GOOD TO DRINK
   C. MADE A MESS

61

MULTIPLE CHOICE

CIRCLE THE CORRECT ANSWER.

1. WHAT WAS GIVEN TO PAUL TO KEEP HIM HUMBLE? 2 CORINTHIANS 12:7
   A. A THORN IN THE FLESH
   B. BLINDNESS
   C. POVERTY

2. FOR WHAT DID ESAU SELL HIS BIRTHRIGHT? GENESIS 25:34
   A. HAMBURGER AND FRIES
   B. A BOWL OF STEW
   C. A NEW SUIT OF CLOTHES

3. HAVE DID JESUS SAY THE RICH MAN MUST SELL TO HAVE TREASURES IN HEAVEN? MATTHEW 19:21
   A. HIS HOUSE
   B. ALL HIS POSSESSIONS
   C. HIS BROTHER

62

CONT'D FROM PREVIOUS PAGE.

4. WHAT WAS FOUND IN BENJAMIN'S PACK? GENESIS 44:12
   A. A FROG
   B. HIS CLOTHES
   C. JOSEPH'S SILVER CUP

5. WHAT KIND OF TREE DID JESUS CONDEMN? MARK 11:14
   A. AN APPLE TREE
   B. A FIG TREE
   C. A PLUM TREE

6. WHAT PARABLE TELLS OF THE SON THAT LEAVES HOME AND WASTED ALL HIS MONEY? LUKE 15:11-32
   A. THE WANDERING SON
   B. ONE FREE SON
   C. THE PRODIGAL SON

OUCH!

63

FILL IN THE BLANKS

WORD LIST

DEEPLY	HOMES
LOOKING	OTHERS'
COMPLAINING	EACH
OPEN	LOVE

" MOST IMPORTANTLY, _LOVE_ EACH OTHER _DEEPLY_. LOVE HAS A WAY OF NOT _LOOKING_ AT _OTHERS'_ SINS _OPEN_ YOUR _HOMES_ TO _EACH_ OTHER WITHOUT _COMPLAINING_."

64

FILL IN THE BLANKS

WORD LIST

GIFT	GRACE
DIFFERENT	RESPONSIBLE
SERVANTS	YOU
GOD'S	EACH

" _EACH_ OF YOU RECEIVED A SPIRITUAL _GIFT_ GOD HAS SHOWN YOU HIS _GRACE_ IN GIVING YOU _DIFFERENT_ GIFTS AND _YOU_ ARE LIKE _SERVANTS_ WHO ARE _RESPONSIBLE_ FOR USING _GOD'S_ GIFTS."

65

READ 2 PETER 1:5-7. WHAT SHOULD YOU ADD TO EACH QUALITY BELOW?

LOOK ON THE FOLLOWING PAGE FOR YOUR ANSWERS.

FAITH	GOODNESS
GOODNESS	KNOWLEDGE
KNOWLEDGE	SELF-CONTROL
SELF-CONTROL	ABILITY TO HOLD ON
ABILITY TO HOLD ON	SERVICE TO GOD
SERVICE TO GOD	BROTHERLY KINDNESS
BROTHERLY KINDNESS	LOVE

THIS SCRIPTURE CONTINUES IN VERSES 8-9.

" IF ALL THESE THINGS ARE IN YOU AND ARE GROWING, THEY WILL HELP YOU NEVER TO BE USELESS. THEY WILL HELP YOUR KNOWLEDGE OF OUR LORD JESUS CHRIST AND MAKE YOUR LIVES BETTER. BUT IF ANYONE DOES NOT HAVE THESE THINGS, HE CANNOT SEE CLEARLY. HE IS BLIND. HE HAS FORGOTTEN THAT HE WAS MADE CLEAN FROM HIS PAST SINS."

WHAT A GREAT PROMISE!

66

MATCH THE COLUMNS

WHO WAS WHOSE WIFE?

DRAW A LINE TO MATCH HUSBAND TO WIFE.

ABRAHAM — RUTH
BOAZ — PRISCILLA
DAVID — HERODIAS
KING XERXES — BATHSHEBA
ELKANAH — ESTHER
HEROD — HANNAH
AQUILA — SARAH

68

TRUE / FALSE

1. JOSEPH WAS TWENTY-THREE YEARS OLD WHEN HIS BROTHERS SOLD HIM TO THE ISHMAELITES.

   TRUE ___ FALSE ✓

2. LAZARUS HAD BEEN DEAD FOR THREE DAYS WHEN JESUS CALLED HIM OUT OF HIS TOMB, RAISING HIM TO LIFE.

   TRUE ___ FALSE ✓

3. MOSES AND ABRAHAM APPEARED WITH JESUS ON THE NIGHT OF TRANSFIGURATION.

   TRUE ___ FALSE ✓

4. JESUS FED FOUR THOUSAND PEOPLE WITH A FEW LOAVES OF BREAD AND SOME FISH.

   TRUE ✓ FALSE ___

69

MULTIPLE CHOICE

CIRCLE THE CORRECT ANSWER.

1. HE WANTED TO PUT HIS HAND IN JESUS' SIDE AFTER HIS RESURRECTION.

   A. THOMAS
   B. JOHN
   C. PETER

2. JESUS CALLED HIM AWAY FROM HIS JOB AS A TAX COLLECTOR.

   A. PHILIP
   B. MATTHEW
   C. JAMES

3. JESUS HEALED HIS MOTHER-IN-LAW.

   A. JOHN
   B. JAMES
   C. PETER

CONT'D NEXT PAGE...

70

...CONT'D FROM PREVIOUS PAGE.

d. HE GAVE JESUS A KISS, BUT NOT OUT OF LOVE.

   A. PONTIUS PILATE
   B. JUDAS ISCARIOT
   C. JOHN

e. HE BAPTIZED AN ETHIOPIAN HE MET ON THE ROAD.

   A. PHILIP
   B. SIMON
   C. ANDREW

f. HE AND HIS BROTHER LEFT THEIR FATHER TO FOLLOW JESUS.

   A. PETER
   B. THOMAS
   C. JUDAS

71

FINISH THE VERSE

HERE ARE SOME OF THE BEATITUDES. FINISH THEM BY MATCHING THEM WITH THE PHRASES ON THE FOLLOWING PAGE.

1. "BLESSED ARE THE POOR IN SPIRIT" "THEIRS IS THE KINGDOM OF HEAVEN."

2. "BLESSED ARE THOSE WHO MOURN" "THEY WILL BE COMFORTED."

3. "BLESSED ARE THE MEEK." "THEY WILL INHERIT THE EARTH."

4. "BLESSED ARE THOSE WHO HUNGER AND THIRST FOR RIGHTEOUSNESS." "THEY WILL BE FILLED."

5. "BLESSED ARE THE MERCIFUL." "THEY WILL BE SHOWN MERCY."

6. "BLESSED ARE THE PEACEMAKERS." "THEY WILL BE CALLED SONS OF GOD."

(SEE INSTRUCTIONS ABOVE)

72

MATCH THE SAYING

MATCH THE SAYING BELOW WITH THE PERSON WHO SAID IT FROM THE FOLLOWING PAGE.

1. "YOUR FATHER AND I WERE VERY WORRIED ABOUT YOU. WE HAVE BEEN LOOKING FOR YOU."

   MARY, HIS MOTHER

2. "I SINNED. I GAVE YOU AN INNOCENT MAN TO BE KILLED."

   JUDAS ISCARIOT

3. "AS FOR ME AND MY FAMILY, WE WILL SERVE THE LORD."

   JOSHUA

4. "NO! I WANT CAESAR TO HEAR MY CASE!"

   PAUL

5. "I HAVE SINNED AGAINST THE LORD."

   DAVID

74

FILL IN THE BLANKS

WORD LIST

ANSWER	MORNING
GOD	CRY
WAIT	YOU
NEED	VOICE

"LISTEN TO MY **CRY** FOR HELP, MY KING AND MY **GOD**. I PRAY TO **YOU**, LORD. EVERY **MORNING** YOU HEAR MY **VOICE**. EVERY MORNING I TELL YOU WHAT I **NEED**. AND I **WAIT** FOR YOUR **ANSWER**."

PSALM 5:2-3

76

FILL IN THE BLANKS

WORD LIST

TIRED	WORK
HEAVY	SOULS
REST	EASY
LOADS	LEARN

"COME TO ME, ALL OF YOU WHO ARE **TIRED** AND HAVE HEAVY **LOADS**. I WILL GIVE YOU **REST**. ACCEPT MY **WORK** AND **LEARN** FROM ME. I AM GENTLE AND HUMBLE IN SPIRIT. AND YOU WILL FIND REST FOR YOUR **SOULS**. THE WORK I ASK YOU TO ACCEPT IS **EASY**. THE LOAD I GIVE YOU TO CARRY IS NOT **HEAVY**."

MATTHEW 11:28-30

77

MULTIPLE CHOICE
CIRCLE THE CORRECT ANSWER.

1. HOW MANY TIMES DID JOSEPH AND MARY RUN FOR THEIR LIVES WITH JESUS?
   Matthew 2:13-23
   - (A) ONCE
   - B. TWICE
   - C. THREE TIMES

2. HOW MANY DAYS DID GOD GIVE THE PEOPLE OF NINEVEH TO TURN FROM THEIR SIN OR THEY WOULD BE DESTROYED?
   Jonah 3:4
   - A. SEVEN DAYS
   - (B) FORTY DAYS
   - C. TWENTY DAYS

3. HOW LONG DID IT GO NO WITHOUT RAINING AFTER ELIJAH PRAYED?
   Luke 4:25
   - A. TWO AND A HALF DAYS
   - B. THREE AND A HALF DAYS
   - (C) THREE AND A HALF YEARS

CONT'D NEXT PAGE...

78

(continued from previous page)

4. HOW MANY PEOPLE DID KING NEBUCHADNEZZAR SEE WALKING IN THE FURNACE?
   Daniel 3:25
   - A. THREE
   - (B) FOUR
   - C. FIVE

5. HOW MANY BROTHERS DID JESUS HAVE?
   Mark 6:3
   - A. NONE
   - B. TWO
   - (C) FOUR

6. WHICH PLAGUE ON EGYPT INVOLVED HAIL AND FIRE?
   Exodus 9:23-26
   - A. THE THIRD
   - B. THE FIFTH
   - (C) THE SEVENTH

79

MULTIPLE CHOICE
CIRCLE THE CORRECT ANSWER.

1. HOW OLD WAS JESUS WHEN HE WAS BAPTIZED AND STARTED HIS MINISTRY?
   Luke 3:21-23
   - A. ABOUT NINETEEN
   - B. ABOUT TWENTY-FIVE
   - (C) ABOUT THIRTY

2. HOW LONG WAS MOSES ON THE MOUNTAIN TO RECEIVE THE TEN COMMANDMENTS?
   Exodus 24:18
   - A. OVERNIGHT
   - B. FORTY DAYS
   - (C) FORTY DAYS AND NIGHTS

3. WHEN HE WAS PRAYING, HOW MANY TIMES DID JESUS WAKE HIS DISCIPLES IN THE GARDEN OF GETHSEMANE?
   Matthew 26:36-46
   - A. ONCE
   - B. TWICE
   - (C) THREE TIMES

CONT'D NEXT PAGE...

80

(continued from previous page)

4. WHAT KIND OF CLOTHING DID THE SOLDIERS MAKE JESUS WEAR?
   Matthew 27:28
   - A. A WHITE ROBE
   - (B) A PURPLE ROBE
   - C. A BLUE ROBE

5. WHAT WOMAN LED AN ARMY INTO BATTLE?
   Judges 4:4-9
   - A. RUTH
   - (B) DEBORAH
   - C. ESTHER

6. WHAT OTHER NAME WERE THE WISE MEN CALLED?
   Matthew 2:1
   - A. WISE MEN
   - B. KINGS
   - (C) MAGI

81

MATCH THE ANSWERS
MATCH THE ANSWERS ON THE FOLLOWING PAGE TO THE QUESTIONS BELOW.

1. ON HIS THIRD MISSIONARY JOURNEY, WHERE WAS PAUL ARRESTED?
   JERUSALEM
   Acts 21:30-33

2. HOW MANY BASKETS OF BREAD WERE LEFT AFTER JESUS FED THE FOUR THOUSAND?
   SEVEN BASKETS
   Matthew 15:34-37

3. WHO BROUGHT JUDAS, A DISCIPLE OF JESUS, BACK TO LIFE?
   PETER
   Acts 20:9-11

4. WHO DID KING DAVID SEND TO THE FRONT LINE SO THAT HE WOULD BE KILLED IN BATTLE?
   URIAH
   2 Samuel 11:14-17

5. WHO WANTED JESUS' TOMB SEALED AND GUARDED SO NO ONE COULD STEAL THE BODY?
   PHARISEES
   Matthew 27:62-66

6. WHO THREATENED TO KILL ALL THE BELIEVERS OF JESUS?
   SAUL
   Acts 9:1

82

TRUE / FALSE

1. THE BOOK OF EXODUS RECORDS THAT JOSEPH DIED WHEN HE WAS 100 AND WAS BURIED AND TEN YEARS OLD.
   Genesis 50:26 TRUE **✓** FALSE ___

2. MOSES WAS ABRAHAM'S FATHER.
   Exodus 6:20 TRUE ___ FALSE **✓**

3. HAM, THE SON OF NOAH, HAD FOUR SONS.
   Genesis 10:6 TRUE **✓** FALSE ___

4. PONTIUS PILATE ORDERED THREE SOLDIERS TO GUARD JESUS' TOMB.
   Matthew 27:66 TRUE ___ FALSE **✓**

5. JONATHAN WAS SAMUEL'S SON.
   1 Samuel 14:49 TRUE ___ FALSE **✓**

84

TRUE / FALSE

1. JESUS WAS BORN IN JERUSALEM.
   Matthew 2:1 TRUE ___ FALSE **✓**

2. THE THREE WISE MEN RETURNED TO KING HEROD WITH INFORMATION ABOUT JESUS.
   Matthew 2:12 TRUE ___ FALSE **✓**

3. JESUS WAS CALLED A NAZARENE BECAUSE HE LIVED IN THE TOWN OF NAZARETH.
   Matthew 2:23 TRUE **✓** FALSE ___

4. PETER BETRAYED JESUS TO THE LORD AND SAID HE WOULD.
   John 18:26 TRUE ___ FALSE **✓**

5. GOLIATH WAS AN ISRAELITE AND A FRIEND OF THE YOUNG DAVID.
   1 Samuel 17:4 TRUE ___ FALSE **✓**

85

TRUE / FALSE

1. KING SAUL WANTED TO KILL DAVID BECAUSE OF HIS JEALOUSY.
   1 SAMUEL 19:1   TRUE ✓ FALSE ___

2. NOAH LIVED FOR NINE HUNDRED AND THIRTY-FIVE YEARS.
   GENESIS 9:29   TRUE ___ FALSE ✓

3. AT FIRST, JOSEPH FELT HE SHOULD DIVORCE MARY WHEN HE FOUND OUT SHE WAS PREGNANT.
   MATTHEW 1:19   TRUE ✓ FALSE ___

4. JESUS' FATHER, JOSEPH, WAS A SON OF DAVID.
   MATTHEW 1:20   TRUE ✓ FALSE ___

5. EMMANUEL MEANS "GOD WITH US" AND IS ANOTHER NAME FOR JESUS FROM THE OLD TESTAMENT.
   MATTHEW 1:23   TRUE ✓ FALSE ___
   ISAIAH 7:14

86

MATCH THE SAYING

MATCH THE SAYING BELOW WITH THE PERSON WHO SAID IT FROM THE FOLLOWING PAGE.

1. " THIS PUNISHMENT IS MORE THAN I CAN STAND ! "   GENESIS 4:13
   __CAIN__

2. " THERE IS ONLY ONE GOD, AND THERE IS ONLY ONE WAY THAT PEOPLE CAN REACH GOD "   1 TIMOTHY 2:5
   __PAUL__

3. " BUT THE MOST HIGH GOD NOT LIVE IN HOUSES THAT MEN BUILD WITH THEIR HANDS! "   ACTS 7:48
   __STEPHEN__

4. " SEE, TODAY I AM LETTING YOU CHOOSE A BLESSING OR A CURSE. "   DEUTERONOMY 11:26
   __MOSES__

5. " AS SURELY AS THE LORD LIVES, DAVID WON'T BE PUT TO DEATH. "   1 SAMUEL 19:6
   __SAUL__

87

TRUE / FALSE

1. LOT WAS THE SON OF ABRAHAM.
   GENESIS 11:31   TRUE ___ FALSE ✓

2. SAUL WAS NOT JONATHAN'S FATHER. HE WAS DAVID'S FATHER.
   1 SAMUEL 19:1   TRUE ___ FALSE ✓

3. JONATHAN DID NOT LIKE DAVID AND WANTED NOTHING TO DO WITH HIM.
   1 SAMUEL 19:1   TRUE ___ FALSE ✓

4. SHEM, NOAH'S SON, HAD AN OLDER BROTHER NAMED JAPHETH.
   GENESIS 10:21   TRUE ✓ FALSE ___

5. MANY DAYS PLEADED, OR BEGGED, TO MARRY JOSEPH.
   MATTHEW 1:18   TRUE ___ FALSE ✓

89

MULTIPLE CHOICE

CIRCLE THE CORRECT ANSWER.

1. WHO WAS JACOB'S FIRST SON ?   GENESIS 49:3
   A. ESAU
   B. REUBEN
   C. ISAAC

2. HOW MANY SONS DID TERAH HAVE ?   GENESIS 11:26
   A. ONE
   B. TWO
   C. THREE

3. WHAT WAS NIMROD KNOWN AS ?   GENESIS 10:9
   A. A GREAT WARRIOR
   B. A GREAT FARMER
   C. A GREAT HUNTER

90

... CON'T FROM PREVIOUS PAGE .

4. WHAT WAS THE NAME OF SAMUEL'S FIRSTBORN SON ?   1 SAMUEL 8:2
   A. ABIJAH
   B. JOEL
   C. SAMUEL, JR.

5. HOW DID PETER ESCAPE FROM PRISON ?   ACTS 12:7-10
   A. HE DRILLED HIS WAY OUT.
   B. HIS FRIENDS HID A FILE IN A CAKE.
   C. AN ANGEL OF THE LORD GOT HIM OUT.

6. WHAT IS ONE OF THE FOUR LIVING CREATURES IN THE VISION OF HEAVEN ?   REVELATION 4:7
   A. A CAT
   B. AN EAGLE
   C. A SNAKE

91

MULTIPLE CHOICE

CIRCLE THE CORRECT ANSWER.

1. WHO WROTE THE BOOK OF EPHESIANS IN THE NEW TESTAMENT ?   EPHESIANS 1:1
   A. EPHESIA
   B. TIMOTHY
   C. PAUL

2. HOW MANY LOAVES OF BREAD AND FISH DID JESUS USE TO FEED THE FOUR THOUSAND ?   MATTHEW 15:34
   A. THREE LOAVES OF BREAD AND SEVEN FISH
   B. SEVEN LOAVES OF BREAD AND A FEW FISH
   C. FOUR THOUSAND LOAVES OF BREAD AND FOUR THOUSAND FISH

3. THE SECOND PLAGUE ON EGYPT WAS...?   EXODUS 8:1-15
   A. FROGS
   B. LOCUSTS
   C. FLIES

92

... CON'T FROM PREVIOUS PAGE .

4. HOW DID SAUL KILL HIMSELF ?   1 SAMUEL 31:4
   A. RAN HIMSELF
   B. FELL ON A SWORD
   C. ASKED HIS SERVANT TO DO IT

5. HOW DID GOD GUARD THE WAY TO THE TREE OF LIFE ?   GENESIS 3:24
   A. PUT DOGS AROUND IT
   B. MADE IT INVISIBLE
   C. SENT CHERUBIMS AND A FLAMING SWORD

6. HOW DID GOD CREATE THE FIRST WOMAN ?   GENESIS 2:21-22
   A. OUT OF DUST
   B. OUT OF ADAM'S RIB
   C. OUT OF ADAM'S SHOULDER

93

FILL IN THE BLANKS

WORD LIST	
MYSELF	WORK
DESIRED	PLEASED
REWARD	ANY
MISS	WANTED

" ANYTHING I SAW AND __WANTED__, I GOT FOR __MYSELF__. I DID NOT __MISS__ __ANY__ PLEASURE I __DESIRED__. I WAS __PLEASED__ WITH EVERYTHING I DID. AND THIS PLEASURE WAS THE __REWARD__ FOR ALL MY HARD __WORK__. "   ECCLESIASTES 2:10

94

FILL IN THE BLANKS

WORD LIST	
WHAT	GAIN
JUST	I
WIND	HARD
CHASING	TIME

" BUT THEN __I__ LOOKED AT __WHAT__ I HAD DONE. I THOUGHT ABOUT ALL THE __HARD__ WORK. SUDDENLY I REALIZED IT WAS __JUST__ A WASTE OF __TIME__, LIKE __CHASING__ THE __WIND__! THERE IS NOTHING TO __GAIN__ FROM ANYTHING WE DO HERE ON EARTH. "   ECCLESIASTES 2:11

95

FILL IN THE BLANKS

" NOW EVERYTHING HAS
BEEN HEARD . HERE
IS MY FINAL ADVICE
HONOR GOD AND
OBEY HIS
COMMANDS THIS
IS THE MOST IMPORTANT
THING PEOPLE CAN
DO "

ECCLESIASTES 12.13

96

FILL IN THE BLANKS

" WE KNOW THAT IN
EVERYTHING
GOD WORKS FOR THE
GOOD OF THOSE WHO LOVE
HIM THEY ARE THE
PEOPLE GOD
CALLED, BECAUSE THAT WAS
HIS PLAN "

ROMANS 8.28

97

MATCH THE SAYING

MATCH THE SAYING BELOW WITH THE
PERSON WHO SAID IT FROM THE
FOLLOWING PAGE.

1. " I COME AGAINST YOU IN THE NAME OF
THE LORD ALMIGHTY "
DAVID   1 Samuel 17 45

2. " MANY WHO HAVE THE HIGHEST PLACE
NOW WILL HAVE THE LOWEST PLACE
IN THE FUTURE "
JESUS   MARK 10.31

3. " TO THOSE WHO ARE PURE ALL
THINGS ARE PURE "
PAUL   Titus 1.15

4. " COME HERE I'LL FEED YOUR BODY
TO THE BIRDS OF THE AIR AND THE
WILD ANIMALS "
GOLIATH   1 Samuel 17 44

5. " LOOK ! I SEE HEAVEN OPEN AND I SEE THE
SON OF MAN STANDING AT GOD'S RIGHT SIDE "
STEPHEN   ACTS 7 56

98

ANSWER PAGES

FILL IN THE BLANKS

WHY THE BOOK OF PROVERBS IS IMPORTANT TO READ

"THEY **TEACH** WISDOM AND SELF- **CONTROL** . THEY GIVE UNDERSTANDING . THEY WILL TEACH YOU HOW TO BE **WISE** AND SELF- CONTROLLED. THEY WILL TEACH YOU WHAT IS **HONEST** AND FAIR AND **RIGHT** . THEY GIVE THE ABILITY TO **THINK** TO THOSE WITH LITTLE KNOWLEDGE. THEY GIVE KNOWLEDGE AND GOOD **SENSE** TO THE **YOUNG** ."

— PROVERBS 1:2-4

WORD LIST	
CONTROL	THINK
HONEST	TEACH
SENSE	RIGHT
WISE	YOUNG

100

TRUE / FALSE

1. SAMSON LED THE NATION OF ISRAEL FOR FIFTEEN YEARS.

JUDGES 16:31   TRUE ____ FALSE ✓

2. WHEN THE SOLDIERS SAW THE ANGEL AT THE TOMB OF JESUS, THEY BECAME LIKE DEAD MEN.

MATTHEW 28:2-4   TRUE ✓ FALSE ____

3. THIRD JOHN IS THE TWENTY-FIFTH BOOK IN THE NEW TESTAMENT.

TRUE ✓ FALSE ____

CONT'D NEXT PAGE ...

101

CON'T FROM PREVIOUS PAGE

4. CORNELIUS' OCCUPATION WAS TENT- MAKING.

ACTS 10:1   TRUE ____ FALSE ✓

5. WE BECOME CHILDREN OF GOD BY PUTTING OUR FAITH IN JESUS CHRIST.

GALATIANS 3:26   TRUE ✓ FALSE ____

6. JOHN THE BAPTIST CALLED HIMSELF A VOICE.

JOHN 1:23   TRUE ✓ FALSE ____

102

MATCH THE ANSWERS

MATCH THE ANSWERS ON THE FOLLOWING PAGE TO THE QUESTIONS BELOW.

1. WHO ASKED, "WHAT CRIME HAS JESUS COMMITTED?"

PILATE   MARK 15:14

2. WHO ASKED WHY JESUS ATE WITH THE TAX COLLECTORS AND SINNERS?

PHARISEES   MATTHEW 9:11

3. WHO SAID, "IT IS NOT THE HEALTHY WHO NEED A DOCTOR, BUT THE SICK"?

JESUS   MATTHEW 9:12

4. WHO SAID "COME HERE, I'LL FEED YOUR BODY TO THE BIRDS OF THE AIR AND THE WILD ANIMALS"?

GOLIATH   1 SAMUEL 17:4-44

5. WHO ASKED, "AM I MY BROTHER'S KEEPER"?

CAIN   GENESIS 4:9

6. WHO ASKED, "WHY HAVEN'T YOU TAKEN CARE OF GOD'S TEMPLE?"

NEHEMIAH   NEHEMIAH 13:11; 13:11

103

MULTIPLE CHOICE

CIRCLE THE CORRECT ANSWER.

1. WHICH PROPHET MARRIED AN UNFAITHFUL WIFE NAMED GOMER?

A. ISAIAH
Ⓑ HOSEA
C. JEREMIAH
(ANSWER FOUND IN VERSE 1:3 OF THIS BOOK SOMEONE.)

2. WHO WAS ABRAHAM'S SECOND SON?

Ⓐ ISAAC   GENESIS 21:1-3
B. ISHMAEL
C. CAIN

3. THE MAGI WERE ...

A. SOLDIERS.   MATTHEW 2:1-12
Ⓑ WISE MEN OR KINGS.
C. SHEPHERDS

105

CON'T FROM PREVIOUS PAGE

4. WHAT DOES THE LORD PREPARE IN THE PRESENCE OF OUR ENEMIES?

PSALM 23:5
A. OUR CLOTHES
B. DINNER
Ⓒ A TABLE

5. IN THE PARABLE OF THE SOWER, WHERE DID THE SEED FALL THAT WAS CHOKED?

MATTHEW 13:7
A. ON ROCKY SOIL
Ⓑ AMONG THORNS
C. AMONG WEEDS

6. WHERE DID LAZARUS, MARTHA, AND MARY LIVE?

JOHN 11:1
A. JERUSALEM
Ⓑ BETHANY
C. NAZARETH

106

FILL IN THE BLANKS

WORD LIST	
LOVED	KINGDOM
BELIEVES	CHILDREN
LIFE	LOVES
BORN	LIKE

1. "FOR GOD **LOVED** THE WORLD SO MUCH THAT HE GAVE HIS ONLY SON. GOD GAVE HIS SON SO THAT WHOEVER **BELIEVES** IN HIM MAY NOT BE LOST BUT HAVE ETERNAL **LIFE** ."

JOHN 3:16

2. "I TELL YOU THE TRUTH, UNLESS ONE IS **BORN** AGAIN, HE CANNOT BE IN GOD'S **KINGDOM** ."

JOHN 3:3

3. "YOU ARE GOD'S **CHILDREN** WHOM HE **LOVES** . SO TRY TO BE **LIKE** GOD."

EPHESIANS 5:1

107

FILL IN THE BLANKS

WORD LIST	
WORLD	TROUBLES
DEFEATED	HAPPY
HAPPEN	WISDOM
GENEROUS	GIVE

1. "MY BROTHERS, YOU WILL HAVE MANY **TROUBLES**. BUT WHEN THESE THINGS **HAPPEN**, YOU SHOULD BE VERY **HAPPY**."
   JAMES 1:2

2. "I TOLD YOU THESE THINGS SO THAT YOU CAN HAVE PEACE IN ME. IN THIS **WORLD** YOU WILL HAVE TROUBLE. BUT BE BRAVE! I HAVE **DEFEATED** THE WORLD!"
   JOHN 16:33

3. "IF ANY OF YOU NEEDS **WISDOM**, YOU SHOULD ASK GOD FOR IT. GOD IS **GENEROUS**. HE ENJOYS GIVING TO ALL PEOPLE, SO HE WILL **GIVE** YOU WISDOM."
   JAMES 1:5

108

MULTIPLE CHOICE
CIRCLE THE CORRECT ANSWER

1. THE SHORTEST CHAPTER IN THE BIBLE IS
   - A. PHILEMON 1.
   - B. PSALM 117.
   - C. TITUS 3.

2. WHO WAS CHOSEN TO REPLACE JUDAS ISCARIOT AFTER HE HANGED HIMSELF?
   ACTS 1:23-26
   - A. JAMES
   - B. MATTHIAS
   - C. ANDREW

3. WHO WAS A "WILD DONKEY OF A MAN"?
   GENESIS 16:11-12
   - A. ISAAC
   - B. JOHN
   - C. ISHMAEL

CONT'D NEXT PAGE ...

109

CONT'D FROM PREVIOUS PAGE.

4. WHAT EVANGELIST HAD FOUR DAUGHTERS WHO PROPHESIED?
   ACTS 21:8-9
   - A. ABRAHAM
   - B. PHILIP
   - C. ZACCHAEUS

5. AT WHAT HOUR OF THE DAY DID JESUS DIE?
   MARK 15:34
   - A. THE THIRD HOUR
   - B. THE NINTH HOUR
   - C. THE SIXTH HOUR

6. HOW TALL WAS GOLIATH?
   1 SAMUEL 17:4
   - A. OVER EIGHT FEET
   - B. OVER NINE FEET
   - C. OVER TEN FEET

110

FILL IN THE BLANKS
EPHESIANS 6:13-17 IS ABOUT THE ARMOR OF GOD.

1. THE BELT OF **TRUTH**.

2. THE BREASTPLATE OF **RIGHTEOUSNESS**

3. FEET FITTED WITH **READINESS**

4. THE SHIELD OF **FAITH**

5. THE HELMET OF **SALVATION**

6. THE SWORD OF THE **SPIRIT**

WORD LIST	
TRUTH	RIGHTEOUSNESS
SPIRIT	FAITH
SALVATION	READINESS

111

WHO WAS HIS MOTHER?
MATCH SON TO MOTHER BY DRAWING A LINE FROM ONE NAME TO ANOTHER.

SOLOMON — RUTH
RUTH 4:13-17

SAMUEL — HAGAR
GENESIS 16:15

OBED — BATHSHEBA
2 SAMUEL 12:24

ISHMAEL — ADAM
GENESIS 4:1

ELIPHAZ — HANNAH
1 SAMUEL 1:20

112

TRUE / FALSE

1. MATTHIAS REPLACED PETER AS AN APOSTLE.
   ACTS 1:24-26
   TRUE ___ FALSE ✗

2. PHILIP BAPTIZED AN ETHIOPIAN EUNUCH.
   ACTS 8:38
   TRUE ✗ FALSE ___

3. THE DEATH OF THE FIRSTBORN WAS ONE OF THE PLAGUES OF EGYPT.
   EXODUS 11:4-6
   TRUE ✗ FALSE ___

4. JESUS SAID A PROPHET HAS HONOR IN HIS OWN TOWN.
   MATTHEW 13:57-58
   TRUE ___ FALSE ✗

CONT'D NEXT PAGE

113

CONT'D FROM PREVIOUS PAGE.

5. WHEN ABRAHAM DIED, GOD BLESSED HIS SON, ISAAC.
   GENESIS 25:11
   TRUE ✗ FALSE ___

6. ABRAHAM WAS TESTED BY GOD.
   GENESIS 22:1
   TRUE ✗ FALSE ___

7. THE QUEEN OF SHEBA CAME TO VISIT SOLOMON SO SHE COULD MARRY HIM.
   1 KINGS 10:1-2
   TRUE ___ FALSE ✗

114

THE TEN COMMANDMENTS
NUMBER THEM SO THEY ARE IN THE RIGHT ORDER.
EXODUS 20:3-17

12 YOU SHALL NOT MAKE FOR YOURSELVES ANY IDOLS.

9 YOU SHALL NOT LIE AGAINST YOUR NEIGHBOR.

6 YOU MUST NOT MURDER ANYONE.

8 YOU SHALL NOT STEAL.

7 YOU MUST NOT BE GUILTY OF ADULTERY.

CONT'D NEXT PAGE ...

115

CONT'D FROM PREVIOUS PAGE.

10 YOU SHALL NOT COVET ANYTHING BELONGING TO YOUR NEIGHBOR.

1 YOU SHALL HAVE NO OTHER GODS BEFORE ME.

3 YOU MUST NOT USE THE NAME OF THE LORD YOUR GOD THOUGHTLESSLY.

4 REMEMBER THE SABBATH BY KEEPING IT HOLY.

5 HONOR YOUR FATHER AND MOTHER.

116

FILL IN THE BLANKS

WORD LIST

LOVE	SOUL
NEIGHBOR	HEART
LORD	MIND
GOD	YOURSELF

" __LOVE__ THE __LORD__ YOUR __GOD__ WITH ALL YOUR __HEART__ AND WITH ALL YOUR __SOUL__ AND WITH ALL YOUR __MIND__ ."

MATTHEW 22:37

" LOVE YOUR __NEIGHBOR__ AS YOU LOVE __YOURSELF__ ."

MATTHEW 22:39

117

FILL IN THE BLANKS

WORD LIST

ADVICE	CHAIN
TEACHING	FATHER'S
LISTEN	MOTHER'S
FLOWERS	LIFE

" MY CHILD, __LISTEN__ TO YOUR __FATHER'S__ __TEACHING__, AND DO NOT FORGET YOUR __MOTHER'S__ __ADVICE__ ."

" THEIR TEACHING WILL BEAUTIFY YOUR __LIFE__. IT WILL BE LIKE __FLOWERS__ IN YOUR HAIR OR A __CHAIN__ AROUND YOUR NECK. "

PROVERBS 1: 8, 9

118

MATCH THE ANSWERS

MATCH THE ANSWERS ON THE FOLLOWING PAGE TO THE QUESTIONS BELOW.

1. WHERE WAS RUTH'S HOMELAND ? __MOAB__ RUTH 1:1-7

2. WHO WAS THE THIRD SON OF ADAM ? __SETH__ GENESIS 4:25

3. WHERE WAS JACOB BURIED ? __CANAAN__ GENESIS 50:12-14

4. WHO SAID, " IF ANYONE IS NOT WITH ME, THEN HE IS AGAINST ME " ? __JESUS__ MATTHEW 12:30

5. WHO WAS HOSEA'S FATHER ? __BEERI__ HOSEA 1:1

6. IN THE GOSPEL OF JOHN, WHO DID JESUS WEEP FOR ? __LAZARUS__ JOHN 11:21-35

119

CONT'D FROM PREVIOUS PAGE

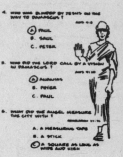

4. WHO WAS BLINDED BY JESUS ON THE WAY TO DAMASCUS ? ACTS 9:3

   A. PAUL
   (B.) SAUL
   C. PETER

5. WHO DID THE LORD CALL BY A VISION IN DAMASCUS ? ACTS 9:10

   (A.) ANANIAS
   B. PETER
   C. PAUL

6. WHAT DID THE ANGEL MEASURE THE CITY WITH ? REVELATION 21:16

   A. A MEASURING TAPE
   B. A STICK
   (C.) A SQUARE AS LONG AS WIDE AND HIGH

124

MATCH THE ANSWERS

MATCH THE ANSWERS ON THIS FOLLOWING PAGE TO THE QUESTIONS BELOW.

1. WHO WAS THE FIRST CHRISTIAN MARTYR ? __STEPHEN__ ACTS 7:59-60

2. WHAT TWELVE-YEAR-OLD GIRL WAS BROUGHT BACK TO LIFE BY JESUS ? __JAIRUS' DAUGHTER__ LUKE 8:40-56

3. WHO GAVE MOSES HIS NAME ? __PHARAOH'S DAUGHTER__ EXODUS 2:10

4. WHO TOLD NOAH TO COME OUT OF THE ARK ? __GOD__ GENESIS 8:15-16

5. IN WHAT TOWN WAS JETHRO A PRIEST ? __MIDIAN__ EXODUS 18:1

6. WHAT WAS THE NAME OF THE CENTURION PAUL WAS HANDED OVER TO ? __JULIUS__ ACTS 27:1

121

MULTIPLE CHOICE

CIRCLE THE CORRECT ANSWER.

1. WHAT HAPPENED WHEN PHARAOH WOULD NOT LET MOSES AND HIS PEOPLE GO ? EXODUS 12:15

   (A.) EVERY FIRSTBORN DIED.
   B. EVERY SECONDBORN DIED.
   C. THE RIVER DRIED UP.

2. TO WHAT DID PAUL COMPARE THE COMING OF "THE DAY OF THE LORD" ? 1 THESSALONIANS 5:2

   A. A ROLL OF THUNDER
   B. A FLASH OF LIGHTNING
   (C.) A THIEF IN THE NIGHT

3. WHAT HAPPENED TO PETER WHEN JESUS ASKED HIM TO WALK ON WATER ? MATTHEW 14:30-31

   A. HE DROWNED.
   (B.) HE SANK FOR LACK OF FAITH.
   C. AN ANGEL CARRIED HIM.

CONT'D NEXT PAGE ...

123

FILL IN THE BLANKS

WORD LIST

SAY	UNDERSTANDING
COMMAND	WISDOM
LISTEN	HEART
REMEMBER	CHILD

" MY __CHILD__, BELIEVE WHAT I __SAY__ AND REMEMBER WHAT I __COMMAND__ YOU __LISTEN__ TO __WISDOM__. TRY WITH ALL YOUR __HEART__ TO GAIN __UNDERSTANDING__ "

PROVERBS 2:1 2

125

FILL IN THE BLANKS

WORD LIST

HIM	KNOWLEDGE
LORD	INNOCENT
HONEST	PROTECTS
WISDOM	SHIELD

" ONLY THE __LORD__ GIVES __WISDOM__. __KNOWLEDGE__ AND UNDERSTANDING COME FROM __HIM__. HE STORES UP WISDOM FOR THOSE WHO ARE __INNOCENT__ LIKE A __SHIELD__ HE __PROTECTS__ THOSE WHO ARE __HONEST__ "

PROVERBS 2:6 7

126

MULTIPLE CHOICE

CIRCLE THE CORRECT ANSWER.

1. WHAT WAS THE FIRST TREE MENTIONED IN THE BIBLE ? GENESIS 2:9

   A. APPLE
   B. CEDAR
   (C.) TREE OF LIFE

2. HOW OLD WAS JOSHUA WHEN HE DIED ? JOSHUA 24:29

   (A.) ONE HUNDRED AND TEN
   B. ONE HUNDRED AND TWELVE
   C. SIXTY-SEVEN

3. WHO WAS MARY'S FATHER-IN-LAW ? MATTHEW 1:16

   A. DAVID
   B. ZECHARIAH
   (C.) JACOB

CONT'D NEXT PAGE ...

127

CONT'D FROM PREVIOUS PAGE

4. WHOSE BONES WERE CARRIED FORTY YEARS THROUGH THE DESERT?
   - A. MOSES'
   - B. JOSEPH'S
   - C. ADAM'S

5. WHAT DID JAMES SAY MAN COULD NOT TAME?
   - A. A BEAR
   - B. A LION
   - C. THE TONGUE

6. HOW LONG WAS JONAH IN THE BELLY OF THE FISH?
   - A. THREE DAYS AND NIGHTS
   - B. SEVEN DAYS AND NIGHTS
   - C. FORTY DAYS AND NIGHTS

128

MULTIPLE CHOICE
CIRCLE THE CORRECT ANSWER.

1. WHY DID MOSES BREAK THE TABLETS OF THE TEN COMMANDMENTS?
   - A. THEY WERE TOO HEAVY
   - B. HE DROPPED THEM
   - C. HE WAS ANGRY AT THE ISRAELITES

2. WHAT WAS THE SIGN OF THE PROMISE BETWEEN GOD AND MAN?
   - A. A RAINBOW
   - B. THE RAIN
   - C. THE ARK

3. WHAT DOES THE NAME "EVE" MEAN?
   - A. MOTHER OF EVENING
   - B. MOTHER OF ALL LIVING
   - C. BEGINNING OF NIGHT

CONT'D NEXT PAGE...

129

CONT'D FROM PREVIOUS PAGE

4. WHAT IS THE FOURTEENTH BOOK OF THE OLD TESTAMENT?
   - A. SECOND CHRONICLES
   - B. FIRST CHRONICLES
   - C. SECOND KINGS

5. WHAT HAPPENED TO THE YOUTHS THAT MADE FUN OF ELISHA'S BALDNESS?
   - A. THEY WERE SENT TO THEIR ROOMS
   - B. THEY WERE MAULED BY BEARS
   - C. THEY HAD TO APOLOGIZE

6. HOW OLD WAS JEHORAM WHEN HE BECAME KING OF JUDAH?
   - A. TWELVE
   - B. THIRTY-TWO
   - C. TWENTY-FIVE

130

UNSCRAMBLE THE VERSE
TO FIND OUT WHAT THE VERSE BELOW SAYS, FILL IN THE BLANKS. ALL THE VOWELS ARE THERE. ALL YOU NEED TO DO IS ADD THE CONSONANTS.

"MY CHILD, DO NOT FORGET MY TEACHING THEN YOU WILL LIVE A LONG TIME. AND YOUR LIFE WILL BE SUCCESSFUL"

"MY CHILD, DO NOT
FORGET MY
TEACHING
THEN YOU WILL
LIVE A LONG
TIME. AND
YOUR LIFE WILL
BE SUCCESSFUL"

PROVERBS 3:1-2

131

UNSCRAMBLE THE VERSE
TO FIND OUT WHAT THE VERSE BELOW SAYS, FILL IN THE BLANKS. ALL THE VOWELS ARE THERE. ALL YOU NEED TO DO IS ADD THE CONSONANTS.

"TRUST THE LORD WITH ALL YOUR HEART. DON'T DEPEND ON YOUR OWN UNDERSTANDING. REMEMBER THE LORD IN EVERYTHING YOU DO. AND HE WILL GIVE YOU SUCCESS"

"TRUST THE LORD
WITH ALL YOUR
HEART. DON'T
DEPEND ON YOUR
OWN UNDER-
STANDING.
REMEMBER THE
LORD IN EVERYTHING
YOU DO. AND HE WILL
GIVE YOU SUCCESS"

PROVERBS 3:5-6

132

TRUE / FALSE

1. MARY, JESUS' MOTHER, WAS NOT AT THE CRUCIFIXION.
   TRUE ____ FALSE ✓

2. JESUS HAD NO BROTHERS OR SISTERS.
   TRUE ____ FALSE ✓

3. ISAIAH WAS AN APOSTLE.
   TRUE ____ FALSE ✓

CONT'D NEXT PAGE.

133

CONT'D FROM PREVIOUS PAGE

4. JESUS WAS TWELVE YEARS OLD WHEN HE FIRST SPOKE AT THE TEMPLE.
   TRUE ✓ FALSE ____

5. BARNABAS WAS A FOLLOWER OF JESUS.
   TRUE ✓ FALSE ____

6. KING DAVID MOVED THE ARK OF THE COVENANT FROM THE HOUSE OF ABINADAB TO THE TABERNACLE.
   TRUE ✓ FALSE ____

134

TRUE / FALSE

1. SOLOMON WAS DAVID'S SON.
   TRUE ✓ FALSE ____

2. DAVID KILLED SIX HUNDRED OF THE ARAMEAN CHARIOTEERS AND THIRTY THOUSAND OF THEIR FOOT SOLDIERS.
   TRUE ____ FALSE ✓

3. ABRAHAM WAS TESTED BY GOD.
   TRUE ✓ FALSE ____

CONT'D NEXT PAGE...

135

CONT'D FROM PREVIOUS PAGE

4. GOD DESTROYED SODOM AND GOMORRAH.
   TRUE ✓ FALSE ____

5. SIMON THE SORCERER BECAME A FOLLOWER OF JESUS CHRIST.
   TRUE ✓ FALSE ____

6. ELISABETH, WIFE OF ZACHARIAS, WAS A DESCENDANT OF AARON.
   TRUE ✓ FALSE ____

136

MATCH THE ANSWERS
Match the answers on the following page to the questions below.

1. WHAT DID EZEKIEL EAT THAT WAS AS SWEET AS HONEY ?
   THE SCROLL _____ Ezekiel 3:3

2. WHO WAS TOLD IN A VISION ABOUT HIS SON'S BIRTH ?
   ZACHARIAS _____ Luke 1:11-13

3. IN WHAT PROVINCE DID JESUS MEET THE FISHERMEN ?
   GALILEE _____ Matthew 4:18-19

4. WHERE WAS JACOB BURIED ?
   EGYPT _____ Genesis 49:29-50

5. WHO WAS SOLOMON'S MOTHER ?
   BATHSHEBA _____ 1 Kings 1:11

6. WHAT IS THE LAST WORD IN THE BIBLE?
   AMEN _____ Revelation 22:21

137

MATCH THE ANSWERS
Match the answers on the following page to the questions below.

1. WHERE WAS JESUS BORN ?
   BETHLEHEM _____ Luke 2:4-6

2. WHAT BABY WAS FOUND IN A BASKET IN A RIVER ?
   MOSES _____ Exodus 2:1-10

3. WHAT WAS THE THIRD PLAGUE THE LORD BROUGHT ON PHARAOH ?
   PLAGUE OF LICE _____ Exodus 8:16-19

4. WHO WAS AARON'S SISTER ?
   MIRIAM _____ Exodus 15:20

5. IN WHAT CITY WAS RAHAB AND THOSE IN HER HOUSE THE ONLY SURVIVORS ?
   JERICHO _____ Joshua 6:17-25

6. IN WHAT MONTH DID THE ARK COME TO REST ON MOUNT ARARAT ?
   SEVENTH MONTH _____ Genesis 8:4

139

MULTIPLE CHOICE
Circle the correct answer.

1. HOW MANY CHARIOTS AND HORSEMEN DID SOLOMON HAVE ?
   _____ 2 Chronicles 1:14
   - A. FOURTEEN HUNDRED CHARIOTS, TWELVE THOUSAND HORSEMEN
   - B. TWELVE THOUSAND CHARIOTS, FOURTEEN THOUSAND HORSEMEN
   - C. TWELVE THOUSAND CHARIOTS, FOURTEEN HUNDRED HORSEMEN

2. WHERE DID ADAM AND EVE FIRST LIVE ?
   _____ Genesis 2:8
   - A. BABYLON
   - B. GARDEN OF EDEN
   - C. ISRAEL

3. WHAT DID PAUL HAVE IN TROAS ?
   _____ Acts 16:8-9
   - A. A COLD
   - B. A DREAM
   - C. A VISION

cont'd next page ...

141

---

cont'd from previous page.

4. THE NAME "ABRAHAM" MEANS ...?
   _____ Genesis 17:5
   - A. FATHER OF NATIONS
   - B. FATHER OF ISAAC
   - C. FATHER OF ALL

5. HOW MANY DAYS DID WATER FLOOD THE EARTH ?
   _____ Genesis 7:24
   - A. SEVEN DAYS
   - B. THIRTY DAYS
   - C. ONE HUNDRED AND FIFTY DAYS

6. HOW MANY PEOPLE WERE KILLED WHEN SAMSON DESTROYED THE TEMPLE OF DAGON ?
   _____ Judges 16:23-30
   - A. THREE THOUSAND
   - B. THIRTY THOUSAND
   - C. THREE HUNDRED THOUSAND

142

MULTIPLE CHOICE
Circle the correct answer.

1. WHAT HAPPENED TO PHARAOH'S ARMY WHEN THEY CHASED AFTER MOSES AND HIS PEOPLE ?
   _____ Exodus 14:26-28
   - A. THEY GOT SAND IN THEIR EYES.
   - B. THEY GOT TIRED OF THE GAME.
   - C. THEY DROWNED IN THE RED SEA.

2. WHAT DID ELIJAH CALL DOWN FROM HEAVEN ?
   _____ 2 Kings 1:10-12
   - A. FIRE
   - B. RAIN
   - C. ANGELS

3. HOW DID JUDAS IDENTIFY JESUS FOR THE SOLDIERS ?
   _____ Matthew 26:48-49
   - A. BY POINTING HIM OUT
   - B. WITH A KISS
   - C. BY A HAND ON HIS SHOULDER

cont'd next page ...

143

---

cont'd from previous page.

4. WHAT LESSON DID JESUS TEACH THE DISCIPLES BY WASHING THEIR FEET ?
   _____ John 13:12-16
   - A. TO KEEP THEIR FEET CLEAN
   - B. TO SERVE OTHERS HUMBLY
   - C. ABOUT CEREMONIAL CLEANSING

5. WHAT DID GOD CREATE TO SEPARATE DAY FROM NIGHT ?
   _____ Genesis 1:14-16
   - A. FIRE
   - B. LIGHTS (STARS) IN THE SKY
   - C. ELECTRIC LIGHTS

6. FINISH PAUL'S SENTENCE "ALL PEOPLE HAVE SINNED AND..."
   _____ Romans 3:23
   - A. ARE NOT GOOD ENOUGH FOR GOD'S GLORY.
   - B. SHOULD BE PUNISHED.
   - C. NEED FORGIVENESS.

144

FINISH THE VERSE
To find out what the verse below says, fill in the blanks. All the consonants are there. All you need to do is add the vowels.

VOWELS : A E I O U

"DON'T DEPEND ON
YOUR OWN WISDOM.
RESPECT THE LORD
AND REFUSE TO DO
WRONG. THEN YOUR
BODY WILL BE
HEALTHY AND YOUR
BONES WILL BE
STRONG."

_____ PROVERBS 3:7-8

145

FINISH THE VERSE
To find out what the verse below says, fill in the blanks. All the consonants are there. All you need to do is add the vowels.

VOWELS : A E I O U

"MY CHILD, DO NOT
REJECT THE LORD'S
DISCIPLINE, AND
DON'T BE ANGRY WHEN
HE CORRECTS YOU.
THE LORD CORRECTS
THOSE HE LOVES,
JUST AS A FATHER
CORRECTS THE CHILD
THAT HE LOVES."

_____ PROVERBS 3:11-12

146

TRUE / FALSE

1. THE LORD CREATED THE GARDEN OF EDEN.
   _____ Genesis 2:8
   TRUE ✓ FALSE _____

2. IT WAS IN THE CITY OF LUZ (OR BETHEL) WHERE JACOB HAD HIS DREAM OF THE LADDER.
   _____ Genesis 28:18-19
   TRUE ✓ FALSE _____

3. LOT PLEADED WITH THE LORD TO SAVE SODOM.
   _____ Genesis 18:16-33
   TRUE _____ FALSE _____

cont'd next page ...

147

3. ADAM PERSUADED EVE TO EAT
FROM THE TREE OF THE KNOWLEDGE
OF GOOD AND EVIL.
GENESIS 3:6

TRUE ___ FALSE ✓

5. A RIVER FLOWED OUT OF THE
GARDEN OF EDEN.
GENESIS 2:10

TRUE ✓ FALSE ___

6. GOD CREATED ALL OTHER LIVING
CREATURES BEFORE HE CREATED
MAN.
GENESIS 1:20-26

TRUE ✓ FALSE ___

148

TRUE / FALSE

1. TROPHIMUS WAS THOUGHT TO HAVE BEEN
BROUGHT INTO THE TEMPLE WITH PAUL.
ACTS 21:26-29

TRUE ✓ FALSE ___

2. TROPHIMUS WAS AN EGYPTIAN.
ACTS 21:29

TRUE ___ FALSE ✓

3. JETHRO WAS MOSES' SON-IN-LAW.
EXODUS 18:12

TRUE ___ FALSE ✓

CON'D NEXT PAGE

149

---

8. AFTER JESUS HAD FASTED IN THE
WILDERNESS, ANGELS MINISTERED
TO HIM.
MATTHEW 4:11

TRUE ✓ FALSE ___

9. THE LAKE OF FIRE IS THE SECOND
DEATH IN THE BOOK OF REVELATION.
REVELATION 20:14

TRUE ✓ FALSE ___

6. PAUL DID NOT VISIT ICONIUM TO
PREACH THE GOSPEL.
ACTS 13:51-14:1

TRUE ___ FALSE ✓

150

MATCH THE ANSWERS

MATCH THE ANSWERS ON THE FOLLOWING
PAGE TO THE QUESTIONS BELOW.

1. WHO ROLLED BACK THE STONE FROM
JESUS' TOMB?
THE ANGEL OF
THE LORD
MATTHEW 28:2

2. IN WHAT CITY THAT PAUL VISITED WAS
THERE A SIGN THAT READ, "TO A GOD
WHO IS NOT KNOWN"?
ATHENS
ACTS 17:22-23

3. WHO HAD A VISION OF A GREAT THRONE
SURROUNDED BY TWENTY-FOUR
ELDERS?
JOHN
REVELATION 4:1,4

4. WHAT WAS URIAH'S OCCUPATION?
SOLDIER
2 SAMUEL 11:10-11

5. WHO WAS THE MOTHER OF KING JOASH?
ZIBIAH
2 CHRONICLES 24:1

6. HOW MANY WIVES DID KING JOASH HAVE?
TWO
2 CHRONICLES 24:3

151

MATCH THE ANSWERS

MATCH THE ANSWERS ON THE FOLLOWING
PAGE TO THE QUESTIONS BELOW.

1. WHO SAID, "LOOK! I SEE HEAVEN OPEN AND
I SEE THE SON OF MAN STANDING AT GOD'S
RIGHT SIDE"?
STEPHEN
ACTS 7:55-56

2. WHO SANG, "GOD FILLS THE HUNGRY WITH
GOOD THINGS, BUT HE SENDS THE RICH
AWAY WITH NOTHING"?
MARY
LUKE 1:46-53

3. WHO CALLED HIS FOLLOWERS "THE SALT
OF THE EARTH"?
JESUS
MATTHEW 5:13,1-13

4. IN WHAT LAND WAS PAUL FORBIDDEN TO
PREACH BY THE HOLY SPIRIT?
PHILIPPI
ACTS 16:6

5. WHAT KIND OF SNAKE BIT THE
APOSTLE PAUL?
VIPER
ACTS 28:3

6. HOW OLD WAS ISAAC WHEN JACOB AND
ESAU WERE BORN?
SIXTY
GENESIS 25:26

153

MULTIPLE CHOICE

CIRCLE THE CORRECT ANSWER

1. DANIEL WAS A...?
MATTHEW 24:15

(A.) PROPHET.
B. DISCIPLE.
C. APOSTLE.

2. WHO WAS MELCHIZEDEK?
GENESIS 14:18
HEBREWS 7:1

A. A PROPHET
B. A MARRIER
(C.) A HIGH PRIEST

3. WHO IS BEELZEBUB?
MATTHEW 12:24-27

(A.) SATAN
B. A PROPHET
C. A KING

CON'D NEXT PAGE

155

---

4. HOW MANY BOOKS ARE IN THE NEW
TESTAMENT?

A. TWENTY
(B.) TWENTY-SEVEN
C. TWENTY-EIGHT

5. WHO WAS HOSEA'S FIRST SON?
HOSEA 1:3-4

(A.) JEZREEL
B. SIMON
C. HOSEA, JR

6. WHAT DID MOSES DO TO GET WATER
OUT OF THE ROCK?
NUMBERS 17:7-6

A. HIT IT WITH A HAMMER
(B.) STRUCK IT WITH HIS STAFF
C. KICKED IT

156

MULTIPLE CHOICE

CIRCLE THE CORRECT ANSWER

1. WHEN THE ISRAELITES WANG OUT
AGAINST GOD AND MOSES IN THE
DESERT, WHAT DID GOD SEND THEM?
NUMBERS 11:31-34

(A.) POISONOUS SNAKES
B. QUAIL
C. MANNA

2. WHAT BROTHERS WERE GIVEN THE
NAME, "SONS OF THUNDER"?
MARK 3:17

(A.) JOHN AND JAMES
B. CAIN AND ABEL
C. PEREZ AND ZERAH

3. JESUS TAUGHT IN PARABLES; WHAT
IS A PARABLE?

A. A BOOK OF MANY STORIES
B. A RIDDLE
(C.) A WAY OF TEACHING BY
COMPARING THINGS TO
GET THE MEANING

CON'D NEXT PAGE

157

---

4. THE NAME "ISAAC" MEANS...?
GENESIS 17:19
GENESIS 18:12

(A.) ONE WHO LAUGHS
B. STRONG AND MIGHTY
C. GRATITUDE

5. WHAT DOES THE NAME "ESAU" MEANT?
GENESIS 25:25

A. BALD
(B.) HAIRY
C. SLIM

6. WHAT TEMPLE DID SAMSON TEAR
DOWN WHEN HE REGAINED HIS
STRENGTH?
JUDGES 16:23-30

(A.) TEMPLE OF DAGON
B. SYNAGOGUE
C. JERUSALEM'S TEMPLE

158

MATCH THE PARABLE

MATCH THE SCRIPTURE REFERENCES
ON THE FOLLOWING PAGE TO THE
PARABLE BELOW.

1. THE WISE AND FOOLISH BUILDERS.
   MATTHEW 7:24-27

2. THE MUSTARD SEED.
   MARK 4:30-32

3. THE PEARL OF GREAT PRICE.
   MATTHEW 13:45-46

4. THE LOST SHEEP.
   LUKE 15:3-7

5. THE PRODIGAL SON.
   LUKE 15:11-32

6. THE WEDDING BANQUET.
   MATTHEW 22:1-14

7. THE GOOD SAMARITAN.
   LUKE 10:30-37

8. THE UNMERCIFUL SERVANT.
   MATTHEW 18:23-35

159

FILL IN THE BLANKS

WORD LIST	
WISDOM	SIGHT
OUT	REASON
LIFE	CHILD
NECKLACE	YOUR

" MY _CHILD_ , HOLD ON TO
WISDOM AND _REASON_.
DON'T LET THEM _OUT_ OF
YOUR _SIGHT_. THEY WILL
GIVE YOU _LIFE_. LIKE A
NECKLACE, THEY WILL
BEAUTIFY _YOUR_ LIFE. "

PROVERBS 3:21-22

161

FILL IN THE BLANKS

WORD LIST	
PEACEFUL	DOWN
NEED	AFRAID
SLEEP	HURT
SAFETY	LIE

" THEN YOU WILL GO ON YOUR
WAY IN _SAFETY_ AND YOU
WILL NOT GET _HURT_. YOU
WON'T _NEED_ TO BE
AFRAID WHEN YOU LIE
DOWN . WHEN YOU _LIE_
DOWN, YOUR _SLEEP_ WILL
BE _PEACEFUL_ . "

PROVERBS 3:23-24

162

FILL IN THE BLANKS

WORD LIST	
KEEP	LORD
PEOPLE	GOOD
HELP	SAFE
TRAPPED	ABLE

" THE _LORD_ WILL KEEP YOU
SAFE . HE WILL _KEEP_ YOU
FROM BEING _TRAPPED_
WHENEVER YOU ARE _ABLE_,
DO _GOOD_ TO _PEOPLE_ WHO
NEED _HELP_ . "

PROVERBS 3:26-27

163

FILL IN THE BLANKS

WORD LIST	
TEACH	GOOD
UNDERSTAND	TELLING
ATTENTION	TEACHING
FORGET	CHILDREN

" MY _CHILDREN_ , LISTEN TO YOUR
FATHER'S _TEACHING_. PAY
ATTENTION SO YOU WILL
UNDERSTAND WHAT I AM
TELLING YOU IS _GOOD_.
DO NOT _FORGET_ WHAT I
TEACH YOU. "

PROVERBS 4:1-2

164

MULTIPLE CHOICE

CIRCLE THE CORRECT ANSWER.

1. RIGHT AFTER JESUS WAS BAPTIZED
   A VOICE FROM HEAVEN SAID WHAT ?
   MATTHEW 3:17

   (A) "THIS IS MY SON AND I
   LOVE HIM. I AM VERY
   PLEASED WITH HIM."

   B. "THIS IS MY SON AND HE
   IS THE WAY TO HEAVEN."

   C. "THIS IS MY SON, FOLLOW
   HIM."

2. WHO ASKED JESUS WHETHER IT WAS
   RIGHT TO PAY TAXES TO THE ROMANS ?
   MATTHEW 22:15-21

   A. HIS PARENTS

   B. HIS DISCIPLES

   (C) THE PHARISEES

3. HOW OLD WAS ENOCH WHEN THE LORD
   TOOK HIM ?
   GENESIS 5:23-24

   A. SIXTY FIVE YEARS OLD

   (B) THREE HUNDRED AND
   SIXTY-FIVE YEARS OLD

   C. SEVENTY YEARS OLD

CONT'D NEXT PAGE...

165

CONT'D FROM PREVIOUS PAGE

4. IN WHAT CITY WAS PAUL ALMOST WHIPPED
   FOR SPEAKING TO THE PEOPLE ?
   ACTS 22:22-24

   A. ROME

   (B) JERUSALEM

   C. MACEDONIA

5. HOW MANY YEARS DID GOD ADD TO
   KING HEZEKIAH'S LIFE ?
   ISAIAH 38:5

   A. FIVE

   B. TEN

   (C) FIFTEEN

6. HOW MANY YEARS DID THE ISRAELITES
   LIVE IN EGYPT ?
   EXODUS 12:40-41

   A. FOUR HUNDRED YEARS

   (B) FOUR HUNDRED AND
   THIRTY YEARS

   C. FIVE HUNDRED YEARS

166

MULTIPLE CHOICE

CIRCLE THE CORRECT ANSWER.

1. WHERE DID MOSES GO AFTER KILLING
   THE EGYPTIAN ?
   EXODUS 2:15

   A. HOME

   B. JUDAH

   (C) MIDIAN

2. MOSES WAS WATCHING A FLOCK OF
   SHEEP WHEN THE LORD CAME TO
   HIM. WHOSE FLOCK WAS HE WATCHING ?
   EXODUS 3:1

   A. THE KING'S

   B. HIS FATHER'S

   (C) JETHRO'S

3. IN WHAT MONTH DID THE ANGEL APPEAR
   TO THE VIRGIN MARY ?
   LUKE 1:26-27

   A. THIRD MONTH

   (B) SIXTH MONTH

   C. NINTH MONTH

CONT'D NEXT PAGE...

167

CONT'D FROM PREVIOUS PAGE

4. WHO MADE HIS WIFE PASS AS HIS
   SISTER ?
   GENESIS 20:2

   A. MOSES

   (B) ABRAHAM

   C. ISAAC

5. WHAT WAS THE POTTER'S FIELD
   KNOWN AS ?
   MATTHEW 27:8

   (A) FIELD OF BLOOD

   B. FIELD OF POTTERS

   C. FIELD OF DEATH

6. WHO TURNED HIS STAFF INTO A
   SNAKE ?
   EXODUS 7:10

   A. MOSES

   (B) AARON

   C. PAUL

168

MATCH THE ANSWERS

MATCH THE ANSWERS ON THE FOLLOWING PAGE TO THE QUESTIONS BELOW.

1. WHO WAS EPHRAIM'S FATHER ?
   JOSEPH

2. WHAT WAS HEZEKIAH'S OCCUPATION ?
   KING

3. WHO WAS THE LAST PROPHET OF THE OLD TESTAMENT ?
   MALACHI

4. ON WHAT MOUNTAIN DID MOSES RECEIVE THE TEN COMMANDMENTS ?
   MOUNT SINAI

5. WHERE DID NOAH'S ARK COME TO REST ?
   MOUNTAINS OF **ARARAT**

6. WHO PLAYED A MADMAN TO ESCAPE FROM HIS ENEMIES ?
   DAVID

169

MATCH THE ANSWERS

MATCH THE ANSWERS ON THE FOLLOWING PAGE TO THE QUESTIONS BELOW.

1. HOW MANY JARS OF WATER DID JESUS CHANGE TO WINE ?
   SIX JARS

2. WHAT OBJECT BROUGHT JOSEPH'S BROTHERS BACK TO EGYPT ?
   A SILVER CUP

3. HOW MANY BOOKS OF THE BIBLE DID JESUS WRITE ?
   NONE

4. AT WHAT AGE DID LAMECH DIE ?
   SEVEN HUNDRED AND SEVENTY-SEVEN

   WHO WAS LAMECH'S FATHER ?
   METHUSELAH

5. WHAT PROPHET WAS COMMANDED BY GOD TO GO TO NINEVEH ?
   JONAH

171

TRUE / FALSE

1. AT THE PASSOVER FEAST, JESUS SAID THAT ONE PERSON WOULD BETRAY HIM.
   TRUE ✓ FALSE ____

2. JESUS RODE ON A HORSE TO JERUSALEM.
   TRUE ____ FALSE ✓

3. JOHN WROTE THE BOOK OF REVELATION WHILE IN ROME.
   TRUE ____ FALSE ✓

173

CONT'D FROM PREVIOUS PAGE

4. BARSABAS WAS AN APOSTLE.
   TRUE ____ FALSE ✓

5. ABRAHAM LEFT EVERYTHING TO HIS SON ISAAC WHEN HE DIED.
   TRUE ✓ FALSE ____

6. BECAUSE ESAU WANTED TO KILL JACOB, JACOB FLED TO HARAN.
   TRUE ✓ FALSE ____

174

TRUE / FALSE

1. IT TOOK ELIJAH JUST ONE TRY TO SET FIRE TO HIS WATER-DRENCHED SACRIFICE.
   TRUE ____ FALSE ✓

2. SOLOMON WAS MADE KING BEFORE DAVID DIED.
   TRUE ✓ FALSE ____

3. AARON DIED ON MOUNT HOR AFTER MOSES GAVE HIS PRIESTLY CLOTHES TO HIS SON.
   TRUE ✓ FALSE ____

CONT'D NEXT PAGE

175

CONT'D FROM PREVIOUS PAGE

4. KING DARIUS HAD DANIEL TOSSED INTO THE LIONS' DEN.
   TRUE ✓ FALSE ____

5. NOAH'S SON JAPHETH WAS OLDER THAN HIS BROTHER SHEM.
   TRUE ____ FALSE ✓

6. JESUS WAS THIRTY-THREE YEARS OLD WHEN HE BEGAN HIS MINISTRY.
   TRUE ____ FALSE ✓

176

WHO SAID ?

MATCH THE NAMES ON THE FOLLOWING PAGE TO THE SAYINGS BELOW.

1. "BUT IF A MAN IS ALREADY OLD, HOW CAN HE BE BORN AGAIN ?"
   NICODEMUS

2. "I AM NOT GUILTY OF THIS MAN'S DEATH. YOU ARE THE ONES CAUSING IT."
   PONTIUS PILATE

3. "YOU WILL NOT DIE."
   THE SERPENT

4. "TEACHER, I WANT TO SEE."
   BARTIMAEUS

5. "HE MUST BECOME GREATER AND I MUST BECOME LESS IMPORTANT."
   JOHN THE BAPTIST

6. "NO! YOU WILL NEVER WASH MY FEET !"
   PETER

177

WHO SAID ?

MATCH THE NAMES ON THE FOLLOWING PAGE TO THE SAYINGS BELOW.

1. "I WILL GIVE HALF OF MY MONEY TO THE POOR. IF I HAVE CHEATED ANYONE, I WILL PAY THAT PERSON BACK FOUR TIMES MORE !"
   ZACCHAEUS

2. "A MAN WAS TOLD ME EVERYTHING I HAVE EVER DONE. COME SEE HIM. MAYBE HE IS THE CHRIST."
   THE SAMARITAN WOMAN

3. "I HAVE SINNED AGAINST THE LORD."
   DAVID

4. "I SINNED. I GAVE YOU AN INNOCENT MAN TO KILL."
   JUDAS ISCARIOT

5. "COME FOLLOW ME. I WILL MAKE YOU FISHERMEN FOR ME."
   JESUS

6. "BUT MAYBE YOU DON'T WANT TO SERVE THE LORD. YOU MAY CHOOSE FOR YOURSELVES TODAY. YOU MUST DECIDE WHOM YOU WILL SERVE."
   JOSHUA

179

MULTIPLE CHOICE

CIRCLE THE CORRECT ANSWER. WHO WAS JESUS SPEAKING TO WHEN HE SAID THE FOLLOWING ?

1. "HURRY, COME DOWN ! I MUST STAY AT YOUR HOUSE TODAY."
   A. ANDREW
   B. ZACHARIAS
   C. ZACCHAEUS

2. "BEFORE THE ROOSTER CROWS TONIGHT, YOU WILL SAY THREE TIMES THAT YOU DON'T KNOW ME."
   A. PETER
   B. LUKE
   C. JUDAS

3. "MARY HAS CHOSEN WHAT IS RIGHT, AND IT WILL NEVER BE TAKEN AWAY FROM HER."
   A. LAZARUS
   B. MARY MAGDALENE
   C. MARTHA

CONT'D NEXT PAGE

181

cont'd from previous page

4. "THE ONLY POWER YOU HAVE OVER ME IS THE POWER GIVEN TO YOU BY GOD."
   John 19:11
   A. THE SADDUCEES
   B. THE PHARISEES
   C. PONTIUS PILATE

5. "PUT YOUR FINGER HERE. LOOK AT MY HANDS. PUT YOUR HAND HERE IN MY SIDE. STOP DOUBTING AND BELIEVE"
   John 20:26-27
   A. THOMAS
   B. PETER
   C. ANDREW

6. "DEAR WOMAN, HERE IS YOUR SON"
   John 19:26
   A. MARTHA
   B. MARY, JESUS' MOTHER
   C. MARY, WIFE OF CLEOPHAS

182

MULTIPLE CHOICE
CIRCLE THE CORRECT ANSWER.
WHO WAS THIS WOMAN?

1. THIS WOMAN POURED EXPENSIVE PERFUME ON JESUS' FEET AND WIPED IT OFF WITH HER HAIR
   John 12:3
   A. MARY MAGDALENE
   B. MARY, MARTHA'S SISTER
   C. MARY, JESUS' MOTHER

2. THIS WOMAN WAS THE ONE JESUS FIRST APPEARED TO AFTER HIS RESURRECTION.
   John 20:14
   A. MARY MAGDALENE
   B. MARY, WIFE OF CLEOPHAS
   C. MARY, MARTHA'S SISTER

3. THIS WOMAN RECEIVED FROM JESUS, THE DISCIPLE JOHN TO BE HER SON
   John 19:26-27
   A. MARY, WIFE OF CLEOPHAS
   B. MARY, JESUS' MOTHER
   C. MARY MAGDALENE

cont'd next page

183

cont'd from previous page

4. THIS WOMAN HAD SEVEN DEMONS DRIVEN OUT OF HER BY JESUS
   Luke 8:2
   A. MARY MAGDALENE
   B. MARY, MARTHA'S SISTER
   C. MARY, WIFE OF CLEOPHAS

5. THIS WOMAN WAS SCOLDED FOR NOT HELPING TO MAKE DINNER
   Luke 10:39-40
   A. MARY, WIFE OF CLEOPHAS
   B. MARY, JESUS' MOTHER
   C. MARY, MARTHA'S SISTER

6. THIS WOMAN'S BROTHER DIED, AND JESUS BROUGHT HIM BACK TO LIFE
   John 11:1-44
   A. MARY MAGDALENE
   B. MARY, MARTHA'S SISTER
   C. MARY, WIFE OF CLEOPHAS

184

FINISH THE VERSE
TO FIND OUT WHAT THE VERSE BELOW SAYS, FILL IN THE BLANKS. ALL THE CONSONANTS ARE THERE. ALL YOU NEED TO DO IS ADD THE VOWELS.

VOWELS: A E I O U

"MY CHILD, LISTEN AND ACCEPT WHAT I SAY. THEN YOU WILL HAVE A LONG LIFE. I AM GUIDING YOU IN WISDOM. AND I AM LEADING YOU TO DO WHAT IS RIGHT."
Proverbs 4:10-11

185

FINISH THE VERSE
TO FIND OUT WHAT THE VERSE BELOW SAYS, FILL IN THE BLANKS. ALL THE CONSONANTS ARE THERE. ALL YOU NEED TO DO IS ADD THE VOWELS.

VOWELS: A E I O U

"MY CHILD, PAY ATTENTION TO MY WORDS. LISTEN CLOSELY TO WHAT I SAY. DON'T EVER FORGET MY WORDS KEEP THEM DEEP WITHIN YOUR HEART."
Proverbs 4:20-21

186

UNSCRAMBLE THE VERSE
TO FIND OUT WHAT THE VERSE BELOW SAYS, UNSCRAMBLE THE WORDS. ALL THE VOWELS ARE THERE. ALL YOU NEED TO DO IS ADD THE CONSONANTS.

"TEEUS OWRDS KEA GTH CREEST OT FLEI OFR SBOUT OWN NFDI RMMT. EYHT GNRID HETLAH TO HEY LIWHOO OBYD. EB VERY FCALLEU TBUGR NANT LND OFKU ORYU TSHUHTUO RUU UORY FSIL."

"THESE WORDS ARE THE SECRET TO LIFE FOR THOSE WHO FIND THEM. THEY BRING HEALTH TO THE WHOLE BODY. BE VERY CAREFUL ABOUT WHAT YOU THINK. YOUR THOUGHTS RUN YOUR LIFE."
Proverbs 4:22-23

187

UNSCRAMBLE THE VERSE
TO FIND OUT WHAT THE VERSE BELOW SAYS, FILL IN THE BLANKS. ALL THE VOWELS ARE THERE. ALL YOU NEED TO DO IS ADD THE CONSONANTS.

"NTOD SEU KYUO UMTOU OT LTBL SLEI. NOOT VERE AYS GUTSIN TTHA EAR NTO BTUE. KEPE YORU VEES UCESGOF NO WTHA SI ITRHE. EEPK LKUOGOI EGHTLSIA URBAA OT AOWH SI DGOO."

"DON'T USE YOUR MOUTH TO TELL LIES. DON'T EVER SAY THINGS THAT ARE NOT TRUE. KEEP YOUR EYES FOCUSED ON WHAT IS RIGHT. KEEP LOOKING STRAIGHT AHEAD TO WHAT IS GOOD."
Proverbs 4:24-25

188

TRUE / FALSE

1. JONAH TOLD THE PEOPLE OF NINEVEH THAT THEIR CITY WOULD BE DESTROYED IN FORTY DAYS.
   TRUE ✓   FALSE ___

2. GOLIATH CHALLENGED THE ISRAELITES THREE TIMES A DAY FOR FORTY DAYS.
   1 Samuel 17:16
   TRUE ___   FALSE ✓

3. ABRAHAM'S SERVANT WENT ALL THE WAY TO MESOPOTAMIA TO FIND A WIFE FOR ISAAC.
   Genesis 24:1-10
   TRUE ✓   FALSE ___

cont'd next page

189

cont'd from previous page

4. DANIEL AND HIS FRIENDS ATE NOTHING BUT MEAT AND VEGETABLES FOR TEN DAYS
   Daniel 1:12
   TRUE ___   FALSE ✓

5. WHEN THE RESIDENTS OF NINEVEH REPENTED, THEY PUT SACKCLOTH ON ALL THEIR ANIMALS
   Jonah 3:8
   TRUE ✓   FALSE ___

6. MORDECAI ACTED LIKE ESTHER'S FATHER, BUT HE WAS REALLY HER COUSIN.
   Esther 2:7
   TRUE ✓   FALSE ___

190

1. LAZARUS HAD BEEN IN THE TOMB FOR THREE DAYS BEFORE JESUS CALLED HIM OUT. John 11:39
   TRUE ___ FALSE ✓

2. JOSEPH WAS TWENTY-THREE YEARS OLD WHEN HIS BROTHERS SOLD HIM TO THE ISMAELITES. Genesis 37:2
   TRUE ___ FALSE ✓

3. BEFORE HIS MINISTRY, JESUS WAS A CARPENTER. Mark 6:3
   TRUE ✓ FALSE ___

191

cont'd from previous page

4. AFTER MOSES WAS GIVEN THE TEN COMMANDMENTS, HE WORE A VEIL OVER HIS GLOWING FACE. Exodus 34:33-35
   TRUE ✓ FALSE ___

5. THE LEVITES HAD TO RETIRE AT THE AGE OF SIXTY-FIVE. Numbers 8:25-26
   TRUE ___ FALSE ✓

6. AFTER SAUL KILLED HIMSELF, THE PHILISTINES CUT OFF HIS HEAD AND HUNG IT IN A TEMPLE. 1 Chronicles 10:8-10
   TRUE ✓ FALSE ___

192

1. WHAT WERE THE LAST WORDS JESUS SPOKE ON THE CROSS? John 19:30
   A. "I AM THIRSTY."
   B. "FATHER, FORGIVE THEM."
   C. "IT IS FINISHED." (circled)

2. WHEN JOSEPH BURIED JESUS, WHO WAS WITH HIM? John 19:38-39
   A. JOHN
   B. NICODEMUS (circled)
   C. JESUS' MOTHER

3. JESUS WAS KNOWN AS A...? Matthew 2:23
   A. NAZARENE (circled)
   B. ISRAELITE
   C. ROMAN

cont'd next page

193

cont'd from previous page

4. WHAT DOES "EMMANUEL" MEAN? Matthew 1:23
   A. JESUS WITH US
   B. GOD WITH US (circled)
   C. FATHER WITH US

5. WHO STAYED WITH NAOMI RATHER THAN RETURN TO HER OWN PEOPLE? Ruth 1:16-18
   A. ORPAH
   B. MOAB
   C. RUTH (circled)

6. WHERE WILL YOU FIND THE BOOK OF GALATIANS?
   A. THE OLD TESTAMENT
   B. THE NEW TESTAMENT (circled)
   C. THE DICTIONARY

194

1. WHO WAS ON TRIAL AT THE SAME TIME AS JESUS? Matthew 27:15-18
   A. BARABBAS (circled)
   B. JUDA
   C. PHARISEES

2. WHERE DID THE DEMONS BEG JESUS TO ALLOW THEM TO GO AFTER THEY WERE CAST OUT OF THE TWO MEN? Matthew 8:31
   A. A HERD OF SHEEP
   B. A HERD OF COWS
   C. A HERD OF PIGS (circled)

3. AFTER JESUS HEALED THE TWO BLIND MEN, HE TOLD THEM TO...? Matthew 9:30
   A. BE SILENT ABOUT IT. (circled)
   B. GO TELL THE PHARISEES.
   C. GO WASH THEIR FACES.

cont'd next page

195

cont'd from previous page

4. WHO DIVIDED THE JORDAN RIVER WITH HIS CLOAK? 2 Kings 2:8
   A. JOSHUA
   B. ELISHA (circled)
   C. DANIEL

5. WHO BUILT A CALF OF GOLD TO MAKE THE ISRAELITES HAPPY? Exodus 32:1-4
   A. MOSES
   B. AARON (circled)
   C. JONAH

6. WHAT WAS ANDREW'S OCCUPATION BEFORE HE WAS CALLED BY JESUS? Matthew 4:18
   A. A CARPENTER
   B. A TAX COLLECTOR
   C. A FISHERMAN (circled)

196

MATCH MOTHER TO SON BY DRAWING A LINE FROM ONE NAME TO ANOTHER

HAGGITH — JOSEPH
RACHEL — ATHALIAH
MEHUJAH — ADONIJAH
ATHALIAH — JUDAH
ESAU — JONATHAN

GOO GOO GOO

197

1. HOW MANY YEARS DID SAMSON JUDGE ISRAEL? Judges 16:31
   A. FIVE YEARS
   B. TWENTY YEARS (circled)
   C. FIFTEEN YEARS

2. WHAT HAPPENED TO THE SOLDIERS WHEN THEY SAW THE ANGEL AT THE TOMB? Matthew 28:1-4
   A. THEY RAN.
   B. THEY SANG.
   C. THEY BECAME LIKE DEAD MEN. (circled)

3. WHAT IS THE TWENTY-FIFTH BOOK OF THE NEW TESTAMENT?
   A. 1 JOHN
   B. REVELATION
   C. 3 JOHN (circled)

cont'd next page

198

cont'd from previous page

4. WHAT WAS CORNELIUS' OCCUPATION? Acts 10:1
   A. A COOK
   B. A TENT MAKER
   C. A CENTURION (circled)

5. PAUL SAID, "YOU ARE ALL THE CHILDREN OF GOD BY..." Galatians 3:26
   A. GETTING BAPTIZED
   B. FAITH IN JESUS CHRIST (circled)
   C. GOING TO CHURCH

6. WHAT MAN CALLED HIMSELF A VOICE CRYING OUT IN THE WILDERNESS? John 1:23
   A. ELISHA
   B. JOHN THE BAPTIST (circled)
   C. JONAH

199

Check out these other

KIDS' BIBLE ACTIVITY BOOKS

from
Barbour Publishing

ISBN 978-1-60260-863-4

ISBN 978-1-60260-864-1

ISBN 978-1-60260-862-7

- 224 pages of fun
- Perfect for rainy days, car trips, and Sunday school classes

Available wherever books are sold.